Edmund H. (Edmund Hamilton) Sears

**Christ in the Life**

Sermons

Edmund H. (Edmund Hamilton) Sears

**Christ in the Life**
*Sermons*

ISBN/EAN: 9783337116569

Printed in Europe, USA, Canada, Australia, Japan

Cover: Foto ©ninafisch / pixelio.de

More available books at **www.hansebooks.com**

# CHRIST IN THE LIFE:

## SERMONS.

WITH A SELECTION OF POEMS.

BY

EDMUND H. SEARS,

AUTHOR OF "THE HEART OF CHRIST," "REGENERATION,"
ETC.

COPYRIGHT, 1876,
BY LOCKWOOD, BROOKS, & CO.

Franklin Press: Rand, Avery, & Co., Boston.

# PREFACE.

MR. SEARS wrote for a previous publication, entitled "*Sermons and Songs of the Christian Life*," a preface, much of which would apply equally well to the contents of this present volume. In regard to his sermons, he stated that he assumed the fundamental facts of the gospel history as premises acknowledged by the congregation; and that he did not regard it as the province of a sermon to try to prove these facts, that task belonging to works of another kind. The sermons were written, not for the press, but for the pulpit; and he did not attempt to revise them to the standard of classical taste, believing that they might by such revision lose in point and directness. This volume has had none of the care which Mr. Sears bestowed on his published writings, every thing being printed just as left by him.

He believed that every Christian should have church relations, and be faithful to them; and he always studied to render faithful service to the denomination where Providence had placed him, not by trying to conform to the average opinions of the denomination, but by trying to grasp and bring forth anew the vital truths essential alike to individual progress and denominational life. In the fulfilment of this high purpose, he often found himself standing almost alone; and this isolation was deeply painful to him. Not that his courage ever faltered. His life was marked by many an act of independence, as fearless and resolute as his declaration from the pulpit that he would not obey the fugitive slave law; and he was ever active in the discharge of all the duties of citizenship, and many times threw his whole influence in opposition to his warmest friends. But few knew how much his independence cost him. He was acutely sensitive, shrinking from an unkind criticism, dreading publicity, self-depreciating, retiring, though not reserved, in disposition. In his latest years, when he most longed for sympathy and fellowship, the deep convictions to which long years of patient study had brought him, and his position as one of the editors of the "*Monthly Religious Magazine*," made him a leader in the contest between the extremes of the denomination with which he acted. His disposition was unswervingly just; and he always took the greatest pains not to misrepresent the views, nor impugn the motives, of any person; but he had a keen eye for the weak points of an argument, and ready powers of debate and satire. How unreservedly

he threw himself into the conflict, the pages of the
"*Magazine*" bear record. He did not escape the
harsh criticism and the misrepresentation that he
expected; but these roused no bitterness in his spirit,
and he never, for merely personal reasons, replied to
any attack. If at times his words seemed sharp and
emphatic, they were the expression of earnest feeling
and strong conviction, never of intolerance nor un-
kindness.

Mr. Sears was best known as a preacher and a
writer on religious themes; but the wide variety of
his studies occasionally tempted him into other fields
of literature, where he always met with some degree
of success. But working always with a definite plan
and purpose, he would spare but little time for any
thing not included in his plan of study. His historical lecture, "*The Saxon and the Norman,*" was
many times delivered, and was well received; and it
is here printed in the hope that it may add to the
attractiveness of the volume.

Mr. Sears was exceedingly fond of poetry; and his
powers of memory, naturally strong, had from his
earliest years, been trained to an unusual degree of
perfection; so that his mind was richly stored with
the best poetry of more than one language. In times
when he was compelled to rest from his severer labors,
his own thought frequently found expression in verse.
A large, perhaps the larger portion of his poems has

never been printed; as his judgment of his work, as well as of himself, was always severe, and his verse was often the revelation of his innermost experience. Several poems already printed, but not contained in any previous volume, have been collected in the following pages; and a few are here for the first time given to the public.

In the original plan of this volume, it was proposed to include a short memoir of Mr. Sears, giving a sketch of his early life, of which he himself once wrote a fragmentary but graphic account. But no man ever more carefully avoided bringing into prominence his own personality; and he needs neither eulogy nor vindication. All that he was, he made himself by systematic and untiring industry, and by concentration of all his powers in lofty aims. If his life has any lessons for others, those lessons are contained in his own words, into which he put his very life. It was a simple life of duty, of unceasing toil and activity, — a life kept unspotted from the world, and consecrated without reserve to high and unselfish ends. During his last long and painful illness, he said that he had finished nearly all the work he had ever planned. If his life were spared, he saw plenty of work that he might do, but he did not wish to stay here, and live an idle life, nor to be a care to others. In the year 1862 he was very sick, and doubtful of recovery. His calm resignation at that time, is shown by his verses written then, "*Away from Church.*" But he had plans for work which would, as he thought, require from ten to fifteen years of active life; and he would be glad to stay, and complete it. His prayer had been answered, and he would not again ask for longer life. So his work was finished; and very weak, and suffering much in body, but with intellectual powers undimmed, and with trustful spirit, he lay waiting for the summons to a higher life. A few hours before his death, when his physical agony was sore, and his faculties of speech and hearing were failing, he was asked by one of those around him, if he wanted any thing. With great effort, he spoke one word, "Rest." Soon he passed from that chamber of awful suffering, to find the rest which even they who most loved him here were powerless to give. On the stone above the spot where his worn-out mortal body lies sleeping, are graven the words of the Master to whose cause he gave loving service, — " He that overcometh, the same shall be clothed in white raiment; and I will confess his name before my Father, and before his angels."

# CONTENTS.

## SERMONS.

|  | PAGE. |
|---|---|
| ELIJAH | 1 |
| DAVID | 12 |
| TIBNI AND OMRI | 23 |
| PILATE | 33 |
| THE GOURD | 43 |
| SPIRITUAL RESURRECTION | 54 |
| CONVERSION | 65 |
| SELF-CONSECRATION | 75 |
| CONDITIONS OF SPIRITUAL PROGRESS | 86 |
| SUCCESS | 97 |
| THE THREE ADVENTS | 112 |
| PROGRESS | 127 |
| THE THRONES IN HEAVEN | 140 |
| PEACE BY POWER | 150 |
| THE ATONEMENT | 161 |
| THE TRINITY | 171 |
| THE DIVINE FRIENDSHIPS | 185 |
| ENCOURAGEMENTS | 195 |

THE SAXON AND THE NORMAN . . 205

## POETRY.

|  | PAGE |
|---|---|
| EMANCIPATION | 241 |
| "OLD JOHN BROWN" | 242 |
| SONG OF THE STARS AND STRIPES | 244 |
| SONG FOR JULY 4, 1861 | 246 |
| THE HOME GUARD | 247 |
| HOW GOLD MAY BE KEPT BRIGHT | 248 |
| GOLDEN MEAN | 249 |
| SERENITY | 250 |
| OLD ENGLAND AND NEW | 252 |
| ODE FOR THE UNION COLLEGE CELEBRATION | 254 |
| ORDINATION HYMN | 256 |
| HYMN FOR THE FIFTIETH ANNIVERSARY OF THE SETTLEMENT AT WESTON OF REV. JOSEPH FIELD, D.D. | 258 |
| GOLDEN-WEDDING HYMN | 259 |
| A GREETING FROM THE SUNDAY SCHOOL | 261 |
| CALM AT SEA | 263 |
| DIRGE | 266 |
| GUARDIAN ANGELS | 267 |
| IN SICKNESS | 268 |
| AWAY FROM CHURCH | 270 |
| "SHOW US THE FATHER" | 273 |
| TWO SPIRIT WORLDS | 275 |
| MY PSALM | 277 |

# SERMONS.

# ELIJAH.

2 KINGS II: 11: "Behold, there appeared a chariot of fire, and horses of fire, and Elijah went up by a whirlwind into heaven."

MATTHEW XVII: 3: "Behold, there appeared unto them Moses and Elijah talking with him."

MOSES and Elijah talking with Jesus! The names which represent three dispensations, appearing in close relationship at the consummation of them all,—the dispensation of law, of prophecy, and of the gospel which was the fulfilment of the other two. The passages are wonderfully suggestive to us of the connection of events, and the relations which the most distant periods of time hold to each other, if only we could see things from the other side, where in the angelic vision they blend together in harmony.

The history of Elijah the Tishbite is one of the most remarkable portions of the Old Testament narratives. It has furnished the grandest material, not only for the song and the sermon, but for the painter and the dramatist; and the character depicted has been held up as a model to the reformers of all ages.

I propose this morning to unfold some of the lessons which come from this history, — lessons historical, moral, and spiritual.

1. The first pertains to the authority of the record, and the place which the Bible holds amid the changes of human creeds and opinions. Fifty years ago it was taken as the most literal history, even to the going up of Elijah in bodily form, chariot and all, to a local heaven in the sky. This and all the miracles of the Old Testament narratives were taken in the baldest literal sense, from the manufacture of Adam out of clay, down to the preservation of the three men in the furnace of fire. The Old Testament embodied the science, the history, the chronology, the ethics of the times, such as our grandfathers held them, and such as no discoveries, they thought, were ever to change or modify. Then followed an era of research, of criticism, of scientific analysis, and science appears, with a good deal of conceit, penetrates the heavens where Elijah went up, and finds no place for him or his chariot; pushes back the history of man away beyond Adam and Eve; experiments largely on caloric, and finds that the human form cannot exist in a furnace made seven times hotter than red-hot iron. Hence came the disparagement and the neglect of the Old Testament; its history being treated as myth and fable, and its miracles at one with the old mythologies of India or Greece. Such are two

periods in the history of opinion and criticism, — one
the period of blind faith, the other of blind scepticism. A third period has already dawned. Science
— the most *advanced* science, science that penetrates
not only downward into the earth, but upward also
into mind and spirit — has found that the sceptics
knew less about miracles than they supposed; yea,
that when you get through the crust of matter, all is
miracle; and that when the laws of mind as well as
of matter begin to be understood, and all their interblendings and inter-actings, and the laws of the spirit-
world within the natural, science has only begun to
give us the stammerings of knowledge, stumbling on
facts all the while which open the old Bible anew, and
give even to its miracles a sacredness and a significance they never had before. One of the most scientific men of the age — a man whose science goes not
only downward into matter, but upward into mind and
spirit, says, "Nothing is more evident to-day, than
that the men of facts are afraid of a large number of
important facts. All the spiritual facts, of which
there are plenty in every age, are denounced as superstition: large-wigged science takes off its hat to a
new beetle or a fresh vegetable alkali, and behaves
worse to our ancestors than to our vermin. Evidence
on spiritual subjects is regarded as an impertinence,
so timorous are they, and so morbidly fearful of
ghosts. They are attentive enough to a class of

facts that nobody values, — to beetles, spiders, and fossils; but as to those dear facts that common men and women in all time and place have found full of wonder and interest and importance, they show them a deaf ear and a callous heart."

It is the science that only looks earthward, and sees only one class of facts, that derides the miracles of revelation, and thinks the Bible obsolete. By the science that looks both upward and downward, some of the miracles of the Old Testament are not only restored to their place in a system of Divine Revelations, but are looked upon as avouching realities whose sweep and grandeur our fathers in their narrow literalism could hardly have discerned.

2. For the interior and more close relationship between the Old Testament and the New is more apparent. It is Moses and Elijah talking with Christ. It is the three dispensations which they represent, seen as one continuous system of Providence, like the stalk, the branches, and the flowers of the plant, all of them alike essential in producing the golden fruit of the tree of life. The Old Testament miracles and the New often tend to mutual explanation, and flash light one upon the other; showing the former as only gleams through partial openings, which in the new dispensation are more broadly effulgent. You will not fail to trace the analogy between the miracles of Elijah and those of Christ; between the ascent of

Elijah from Mount Carmel and that of Jesus from Mount Olivet; between the imagery of the prophetic narrative, — the chariots of fire and the horses of fire, — and the imagery of Saint John in the Revelation, who describes in vision the agencies of the Divine Providence, — the God in history moving behind the veil of sense and matter. So striking is the analogy, that Strauss has tried to show that the New Testament writers constructed their narrative with the story of Elijah for their model, — that Mount Sinai has its parallel in the Mount of Transfiguration, and that Carmel has its parallel in Olivet.

3. But the character of Elijah as the reformer of his times, standing forth in such bold relief amid the corruptions of his age, furnishes the third important lesson that comes from the narrative. That he is a real character, and no myth or invention, is plain; for no romancer of that age could have invented all the granite that was in him. To understand him well, we must have a picture of the times he lived in. We must know who was Jezebel, and who were the false prophets whom she brought into Judæa to supplant the Hebrew religion and abolish the worship of one God for the worship of Baal. She was a woman from Sidon, where Baal was worshipped, — a woman beautiful and accomplished; but it was the beauty of the tigress, which concealed all subtlety and cruelty. Baal was the sun; and his rites of worship involved

the worst abominations. The blood of human victims smoked upon his altars. Astarte, or the moon, was also worshipped. Her altars were in the groves; and in them the rites of lust were sheltered and made sacred. This was the Sidonian worship, now becoming the established religion of the kingdom of Israel; and four hundred of its blood-stained prophets were fed at Jezebel's table. The prophets of the Lord had been slain, or had compromised, or had escaped for their lives. One prophet stands out as the last embodiment of the Hebrew religion, — one man standing for the truth, against the government and all its retainers who had given in to the gory rites of human sacrifice. The worship of one God, to all human appearance, is about to be extinguished in the blood of his own prophets. To understand the miracles which Elijah now wrought, we must remember what he represents. The agencies of the Divine Providence centre in him, and circle about him. He stands at the point where the influx of heaven itself meets the efflux of hell. The long line of future events, in which are the Christ and his gospel and a world's redemption, hangs now upon his person. It is just that crisis where the invisible armies, which are generally veiled, come partially into view, — where the veil of sense becomes semi-transparent, and gives gleams of the God and his angels, who are always nigh. Numbers become of no account. One man is as good as a million where he stands for a great truth, and is clothed in its authority and majesty; and a whole myriad who represent some falsity of to-day shrink into their contemptible individualism, and the stream of Providence washes them away like sand. This is what makes Elijah stand forth in such bold relief, and all the miracles at his hand take on a divine significance. Even where we cannot verify the literal fact, the miracle loses none of its meaning. That the fire came down from heaven upon *his* altar; that within the wind, the earthquake, and the fire, he heard the still small voice of the Lord, which spake to the inward ear; that years of famine and years of plenty, and showers from the sea, foreshadowed themselves upon his spirit whose ear caught the whispers of the Lord which foretoken what is to be, — all this becomes credible when we reproduce to ourselves the times, and the man who stood as the last embodiment of the Divine Providence. And with what power and grandeur does it clothe him, with what a moral heroism, when he represents not himself, but a great truth in its majesty! Ahab and all the military force of his kingdom are arrayed on one side; the prophet clothed in skins, with a leathern girdle, is on the other. And yet royalty in its fine robes cowers before him; and you feel, on reading the story, that the prophet is king, and the monarch is his vassal. Such is the supremacy of ideas over brute force; and such the royalty of truth, which no meanness of outward attire can ever conceal, but which rather in such disguise shines more in unborrowed splendor.

4. But we come to another and most important lesson which this whole history brings home to us. It is the invisible Divine Protection which is thrown around every one who has a mission in the world, who has a Divine Idea, and tries to live it and put it into action. We talk very crudely, I think, about the dispensations of Providence. The invisible guards, the horses of fire, are about the men who look for the leadings of Providence, and try to follow them. There is no one who has not some mission in this world, some duty to his times, and some Christian work in it; and the doctrine which the text enforces is, that he who works with Providence, works with an invisible army that engirds him, and moves with him. He never works alone. He may seem to come into danger and to death; but the danger and the death are apparent, and not real. The engirding and guiding Providence is with him; while with others it is only the Providence that permits, and finally brushes them out of its way. And yet how often in our noise and bustle and conceit do we ignore these invisible agencies, and claim their victory as ours! We do not see the Lord in the conflict because of the dust we raise about us.

> How silent move thy chariot-wheels
>   Along our camping-ground,
> Whose thickly-folding smoke conceals
>   Thy camp of fire around!
>
> We tremble in the battle's roar,
>   Are brave amid its calm;
> And, when the fearful fight is o'er,
>   We snatch thy victor-palm.

There is no loneliness, no desertion, no solitude, to the man who has not only faith in Providence, but who is doing Providential work at the same time. A great company is with him, — with him for the best and highest purposes, as much as if he saw them. Yea, sometimes at difficult turns he will have a vivid consciousness of the fact; and it is this consciousness which gives to moral courage all the real lustre which it has. If you would have this perception of the invisible presences, and this sense of eternal security, I pray you do not rest merely with a *faith* in Providence. Everybody has that, and has talked it till it is stale. *Do something!* Do something that will bring you within the living stream of Providence, so that it will bear you up on its currents, and, the navies of heaven riding with you, bear you along upon its waves.

5. One more lesson. The light which our subject sheds around the dread fact which we call death is of exceeding interest. That the ascent of the

prophet into heaven was like the ascension of Christ, is very true; and the sceptical critics are so far right. Yea, further, it is like the transition of every good man to immortality. It is plain, if you read the narrative carefully, that the prophet died as other men die: only in his case we have a gleam from the other side through the opening, and see what is beyond. "I pray thee," said Elisha, "that, when thou art taken from me, a double portion of thy spirit may be with me."—"If thou see me when I am taken up," said Elijah, "it shall be so: if not, it shall not be so." In other words, "If, when my spirit leaves its clay, you can see me and follow me, that will show you that you are indeed a prophet like me, and that a prophet's vision has been given you of the things beyond the veil of time and mortality." And so it was. The invisible agencies that had been around him in his fight with wrong and had given him the victory, gave him the victory over death; the horses of fire and the chariots of fire symbolizing the triumph which greets the true servant of God on the other side of the grave. What a rebuke to our timid and halting faith, which peoples the other side with spectres, and this side only with realities! Happy will it be, if, when our work is done, death as well as life shall be within the protecting and guiding Providence which shall make our place of transition like the heights of Carmel.

Let us remember that God has no favored ones; that the laws of his providence are universal and all-pervading, just as active around the humblest individual to-day as around the Elijahs and the Christ long ago; that the Carmels and the Olivets of history only reveal to us the realities that always are, and the helpers that are always nigh. *Do something.* Do something that brings thee within the loving folds of that Providence. Do not stand indolent outside, to be swept out of its way into the darkness and the cold.

# DAVID.

HEB. XI. 32 : "The time would fail me to tell of David."

HE seems to have been made up of two men. He was a man after God's own heart. His kingdom prefigured that of the Messiah, so that Christ is called the Son of David. He was the most inspired genius of the old dispensation; and his psalms are pitched to a strain so lofty and sweet, that they enter largely into the Christian ritual, as if they furnished to all after-ages the richest language for a fervent devotion. But turn back this old history, and who is this man after God's own heart? Time certainly would fail to tell of his crimes, — his treacheries, his murders, his adulteries, his grovellings in the very sty of sensuality. Murder is too mild a word. His butcheries of the Canaanites were so manifold, that when he had killed them off, — men and women, and little children, — his hands were too red to build the temple, and the work was deferred till Solomon's reign. And this is the man who wrote the Twenty-third Psalm : " The Lord is my Shepherd ; I shall not want."

"Green pastures and still waters" reached through crime and slaughter, — that has been the mystery ever since, and has prompted the question, how the moralities of the old Bible are to be reconciled with the pure morality of the new, or, indeed, with the demands of the pure, absolute religion of humanity. Time certainly would fail to tell of David.

At the same time, his history, dark and bright, is bound up together in this old Bible; and it brings to view a feature of revelation which we are very apt to undervalue, and which sceptics, I think, entirely misapprehend. "Why," said an objector, "there are passages in the Bible which would not bear to be read aloud in any decent society." I certainly should hope they never would be. But it does not occur to these objectors, that the Bible is not only a revelation of God, but a revelation of man, — a disclosure, on the one hand, of human nature, opening up its lowest deeps into the light of day; and a disclosure, on the other, of the Divine character and attributes shining down into those deeps, to show their quality, and search out the lowest depravities of man. So there is just this parallelism running through the Bible, and especially the old Bible, from beginning to end. It is a book of human nature, that opens up from the lowest abyss; and a book of prophecies, that pours down into that abyss the splendors of the Divine face, and the denunciations of the Divine Word. What a

Bible human wit would have contrived for us! Like one of the rose-colored novels, all of which could be read aloud, and admired for once, and then laid on the shelf forever.

Time would fail to tell of David; but he is a largely representative man, — one of the most religious men that ever lived, and, withal, the most sensual; the most tender-hearted, and, at the same time, the most cruel; and, as such, he is a lesson to all times and ages. We will open this book of human nature, and draw out some of its lessons, and apply them, and show how the Bible should be used as a help in the religious life.

1. The first lesson is that of devotion divorced from morality, — worship so absorbed in the praise of God as to be oblivious of the rights and the sufferings of men. The possibility of this wide separation between worship and morality is held aloft as a warning, and in contrast with what true worship should be. "Put Uriah in the forefront of the hottest battle, and then retire from him, that he may be smitten, and die." David did not perceive this to be murder, because it was taking the life of another indirectly and circuitously, and in a way that did not violate the rules of war, and the regulations of the army. He would have shrunk with horror at the idea of private assassination; and so he reaches the same end indirectly, with no sense of guilt upon his conscience. It is the

same mistake which moral men and religious men are very liable to fall into. The violation of the neighbor's rights very often goes for nothing, provided the means are circuitous, and not direct; done according to received moral codes, and not by gross personal assault and robbery; done according to law, not against law. If my neighbor has something which I covet myself, I shall not probably break into his house, or waylay him in the dark. I am too civilized for that. I shall rather blind his eyes to the value of things, and get it from him by the rules of trade and bargain, and under the glamour of false appearances, rather than the darkness of the night. And, having largely supplied myself in that way, I shall be ready for a psalm of thanksgiving, "The Lord is my Shepherd; I shall not want." The real nature of the crime is concealed under the complications of the means through which the end is reached; and yet, to Him who looks through all disguises, it is the same thing under a more respectable name. In our civilized moralities we never kill men outright in order to get their money. We build cheap houses, amid marshes and miasmas, and rent them at high rates to the poor, whose families die off by pestilence. And from the fruits of this slaughtering, Christian men lie down in green pastures.

2. And, again, devotion may be so exclusive and absorbing as to preclude all knowledge of ourselves.

We may be so intent on praising God as to leave no room for thorough self-examination ; and then we may fall into the delusion that God is so flattered with our exaltations of his excellencies, that He will not hold us to a very strict account, and we may live in ignorance of what we really are. And without this self-analysis, we may see faults in our neighbors, and even be indignant for what they do, when we practise the same things ourselves, though with some change of circumstance and occasion.

Worship, when genuine, has a twofold office. It draws us up into the Divine communion, and brings thence the light of the Divine Justice searching out all the hiding-places of the heart, thus revealing us true under the light of the Divine countenance. We can praise God, and admire his power and magnificence, and be-sing his glories, without any of this reflex influence that searches out our own sins, and illumes all the pages of our book of life within. Such was David's state sometimes, amid all his psalms and hallelujahs. And while he is in this state of mind, Nathan comes to him with a message. And Nathan supposes a case. It is the parable of the rich man with many flocks and herds, who took the poor man's lamb, the only one he had, and killed it, and dressed it for his table. David's indignation is greatly kindled at such meanness. He was going away, very likely, to write a psalm about it, and would probably have turned

Nathan's touching parable into a splendid lyric for the temple, to be set to music, and to chant the Divine judgment against oppression. But wait a moment, says the prophet. And then he takes the picture, and writes under it "David." And the psalm was turned into a penitential wail, "My soul is full of trouble. All thy billows have gone over me."

3. And here comes another lesson out of these chapters of human nature. We are very apt to fall into the mistake, that it is the grossness of sin that makes it past forgiveness,—the sin that looks palpable like a mountain, and is therefore hopeless and beyond recovery. Yet here was a man who broke nearly all the commandments of the Decalogue, whose name we find in the New Testament numbered among the saints of the Church of God. The history brings to light, and makes conspicuous, one of the distinctions in human depravity. There is crime which flows from overmastering passion, where the judgment is blinded, and the conscience intoxicated without being quenched, when the animal overcomes the man. The moral and spiritual nature is not hardened and fossilized, but only held in abeyance till it can act again. But when it does act, there is remorse, and acknowledgment of guilt, and heart-breaking sorrow, and pity that flows like rain. Such was David in the animal and spiritual man that made him up. It is the tenderness and moral sensibility under the depravity,

— sensibility that the Divine Spirit at length takes hold of to wash the stains of guilt clean away. There is another kind of depravity,— one which comes not from the animal nature, but from a perverted spiritual nature, when, Iago-like, man is turned into a fiend, when evil is put for good, and good for evil, and repentance is impossible because there is no tender spot in the heart to take hold of. These men do not commit crimes half so gross and shocking to the ear, perhaps never commit any crimes, so cunning are they in their methods, and such are the long underground trains of evil where they work out of sight, without any violations of law. These are the sinners who are hopeless, and in whose flinty natures, worn smooth by the impinging truths that pass over them, no pulse is ever felt. We must keep in mind these revelations of human nature in the old Bible to understand aright its punishments and rewards, and the glorious possibilities of the pardoning Mercy. We must interpret in the light thereof the conditions of our own pardon, and those of our fellow-sinners as well. The Sovereign Grace can save the chief of sinners until the conscience is lost, and the sensibilities have turned into stone. This our Saviour calls the sin against the Holy Spirit, or the sin unto death, for which there is no forgiveness. That may be committed without any gross transgression. It is secret, cunning, subtle, pursuing its ends through systematic hypocrisies till the conscience is put out, and the moral nature turns to marble. David's sins were gross but not hypocritical, those of the animal rather than of the fiend; so his compunctions are terrible. His remorse flows like a torrent, and his guilt is washed away.

4. There is another principle of exceeding interest which is fully illustrated in the history of David. His nature was large and many-sided, infested with animal passions in its lower range, and, in its highest range, soaring into the region of song, seizing the most charming of nature's imagery to illustrate the truths of religion, and set forth the sentiment of devotion. Hence he becomes the channel of the Divine inspirations. He is just one of those men who speak wiser than they know. His song sweeps heights that he never climbed; and he became the channel of revelations, both of God and of human nature, which speak to men's condition through all time. Some writers forget, when they undertake to criticise the word of God, that it was given for the very purpose of speaking to our sinful human nature; and, therefore, it comes through those who share most largely in that nature. A seraph from the third heavens never would have come down to the condition of our gross and erring humanity. His song would have floated over us, without touching us. There was a man who lived two hundred years ago, born on

the banks of the Avon, — a man whose experience went down among the grosser passions and vices, but whose genius soared into the clearest and sweetest realm of poesy, — a representative man like David. And hence he has dramatized human life, both in its darker and brighter shadings; has pictured infernal villainy and angelic grace so truly, that, out of the old Bible, there is no such revelation anywhere of the mysteries and possibilities of the human heart. He sung wiser than he knew or ever intended. He never knew what mysteries of heart he was revealing. And so with David, one of the grossest of sinners, and, at the same time, a poetic genius of the highest order. And so the struggle of the spirit in him against the flesh represents the war in all humanity. And the compunctions of sin, and the peace of God after victory, men read over to this day, and find their own experience mirrored back upon them. Even what are called the imprecatory psalms, the curses upon David's enemies, come to mean what he never intended; for his enemies become, in the Christian's experience, the spiritual foes in his own heart. And the whole kingdom of David prefigures the kingdom of Christ. And this David, a temporal king, with his temporal enemies about him, whom he fights, and conquers, and triumphs over, in psalms and hallelujahs, is taken to foreshadow Christ, the spiritual king, and his kingdom, and his victories over the enemies of the soul, — the unbeliefs, the passions, and the lusts, which hinder the full coming of the Lord in his reign on the earth. And so these songs come down to us to chant our moral victories with to-day.

Such are some of the lessons of this history. And this leads me to remark, as to how the Bible should be used as a means of religious life.

We are to discriminate and distinguish always the human and the Divine element, both bound up together in the same book, and in the same characters sometimes, for the very purpose of showing how one acts upon the other, how the clear justice of God tells upon human depravity. There is a wonderful unity in this book. Any one who has read it from Genesis to Revelation, and who sees how one part unfolds from another, leading on the drama of human history under a controlling Providence, will never believe that it was produced by mere human art, or thrown together hap-hazard. He will be convinced that it unfolds under a Divine hand, and within the breathings of a Divine inspiration, though not a verbal one, bringing together just those Divine and human elements which we need most to study, if we would see human nature as it is, its deepest needs, and its abundant supplies out of the treasury of God. No novel that was ever written has such a unity, moves on to such sublime catastrophes, or shows human nature through such ranges of height and depth. Nowhere are the lowest deeps opened up into the sunlight as here. And out of such depths, and on such a line of descent, the Christ appears, the Son of David, clothing Himself in all this inherited humanity, that He might find it, redeem it, and lift it heavenward.

We must take in the old Bible as well as the new, if we would see all that man is, and the power of the Sovereign Grace to create him anew. Use it again, for self-knowledge and personal application. Go to the Christian records for the full consolation and hope of the gospel; but go back to these old biographies and prophecies to find a light flashing down, sometimes into your lowest consciousness, revealing the depths out of which we are all kept by the creative Word and the Sovereign Grace. If you find in this old word depths of depravity almost too shocking to look into, remember they are depths out of which society has emerged through the Christ, out of which it is kept by the power of Christianity, and the Holy Spirit which operates through the truth which it reveals. By the study of this book, old and new, you shall be saved from any closet theories of human nature; and you will see your own hidden life evermore revealed, as in a glass; and you will pray all the more earnestly that that life be hid with Christ in God.

# TIBNI AND OMRI.

1 KINGS XVI. 22: "So Tibni died, and Omri reigned."

THE kingdom of Israel had a succession of rulers who vied with each other in depravity and wickedness. Ambition, lust, cruelty, idolatry, became impersonated in its kings; and a change of dynasty very often turned out to be nothing more than a change from one kind of dominant wickedness to another. When a new king came upon the throne, the hopes and expectations of the people were raised. Now, said they, we shall have a new policy; now the old vices will be reformed, and we shall have a brilliant reign of prosperity and virtue. But it often turned out that the old vices would be reformed, and wane and disappear, only that some new phase of vice would come. Tibni, the son of Ginath, competes with Omri for the throne; and half the people followed Tibni, and the other half followed Omri; but Omri prevailed, and Tibni died and his faction was suppressed. And Omri reigned, and did evil in the sight of the Lord, and walked in all the ways of Jeroboam. And then Omri died, and Ahab his son reigned in his stead. And he did evil, and slew the prophets of the Lord, and set up the worship of Baal. And Ahaziah succeeded Ahab, and he did evil.

And why is all this told us? and of what use is the history of the kingdom of Israel, and its corrupt and idolatrous kings? Simply because these are chapters in the book of human nature; and in turning over its leaves we are very often turning over the pages of its book of life. A kingdom is the collective man, representing, in the complex, the individual man; and it makes all the difference whether the mind itself be the kingdom of evil Ahab, or the kingdom of God. Indeed, the whole kingdom of Judah prefigured the reign of Christ; and Christ is called a king, the Son of David, and his successor, because the earthly type foreshadows the heavenly reality. The human mind — yes, your own mind individually — is a kingdom in itself; and some ruling passion or principle is regnant there over your whole realm of thought, feeling, motive, and action. Every mind has a ruling passion of some sort. It is Ahab, or it is Christ, enthroned within.

Have you never observed in men the changes that are sometimes called reformation, but which are nothing more than the exchange of one bad principle for another? Have you never observed how one vice in a man may be conquered and slain and expelled altogether, only that another vice, more specious possibly, and of better aspect, may succeed to the throne, and reign there instead, while the character has undergone no radical change whatever? It is Omri supplanting Tibni, and then Ahab coming in the place of Omri, and Ahaziah in his place, and so on to the end of the chapter, — a whole series of evil reigns, with no Christ succeeding them, with only the difference that some are more specious than the rest.

1. There was a man who inherited a princely fortune, but who, in the ardor of youthful passion, spent the whole of it in riotous living. Driven out from his inheritance, and wandering as a prodigal on the earth, he cast back longing and sorrowful glances towards the home-mansion, and the green lawns and landscapes that lay around it. And he made a vow: "I will forsake my bad habits. I will reform. I will make money somehow, and win back my inheritance." And he did reform. He became a man of thrift and temperance and self-denial; and he clutched for the largest gains, and found them. And the prodigal young man became the hard-featured trader, who always took the best end of a bargain. And he won back his inheritance, and made its lawns and landscapes more green than ever. Here was self-denial; but it was self denied in one shape, only to be developed in another. The vice of the prodigal had been denied and killed, and cast out; and avarice had come in its place, and had become enthroned over

the whole realm of mind and character. And so Tibni died, and Omri reigned.

2. Again: there are two kinds of worldliness. There is secular worldliness and religious worldliness. There is the worldliness which makes the world minister only to selfish gains and selfish enjoyments; which heaps up riches, only to pamper the bodily appetites and passions, or the love of luxury and the love of show. This is what Paul means by being conformed to the world. Then there is the other worldliness, looking for the future happiness and the future rewards, from motives just as personal and just as selfish. The other worldliness does not regard the future life and the heavenly mansion as an enlarged sphere of usefulness, with enlarged opportunities for doing good, with the elevation and expansion of all the faculties for the errands of philanthropy and charity, with new facilities for alleviating the miseries of God's universe: it looks upon the heavenly life as a scene of lazy enjoyment, where there is no work to be done, but only indolent devotion to be enjoyed, or barren praises to be sung, or golden streets to be admired; while the universe outside heaven is still groaning and travailing in pain. Such is the other worldliness; and it is not rare to find people converted from one worldliness to the other, from secular worldliness to religious, when the whole idea of heavenly happiness is a larger and more complete and more lazy self-indulgence.

What man ever served the god of this world, without convictions borne in upon him, sometimes with overwhelming power, that his grasp on this world is one day to be loosed, that death will unclasp his fingers one by one, that all these accumulations must be left behind, and that another world, with its immortal realities and its scenes of glory or of suffering, will lie about him? But selfish scheming, and the habit of getting the best end of bargains, uncaring who holds the other end, is not the finest preparation for apprehending spiritual things, or the nature of salvation, or the nature and attributes of God. Salvation, after such an education as this, is very likely to be, just as much as any other transaction, a matter of scheme and bargain and selfish policy. It is the old policy of selfishness taking a religious form. It is the balance of debit and credit transferred from the ledger to the spiritual account. It is so many prayers, and so much faith in dogmas, made over to him, and so much foreign merit imputed to him for righteousness; so much ritual, and so much making believe, in order to turn away the wrath of God and his punishments. It is an external title to enter heaven, to be bought and sold. He never dreams, that, before any one enters heaven, heaven must enter him. And so the old selfishness, with all its calculating policy, is transferred to religion, and rules him still, the foundations of character remaining just the same, none of its hard and flinty lines softened down or obliterated. His religion has made him no better, only changed self from one form to another. The god of this world has been given up; but the god of the other world, who comes in his place, is not the Lord himself, but a superstition, whose ruling motive is lurid fear and selfish hope, and whose servitude is quite as slavish as the servitude of this world. And so Tibni dies, and Omri reigns.

3. Again: there is knowledge which is acquired for the sake of higher usefulness, and there is knowledge which is acquired from love of applause or admiration; or, again, for selfish pleasure, not for usefulness in the world, and a better qualification to do our work in it. Education — that education whose prime object is to unfold all our human capabilities, and develop a perfect manhood or womanhood — looks less to the decorations of life than to its body and substance. The female education that fills up the outlines of the woman nobly planned will have prime reference to work more than to ornament, and to faculty more than to accomplishments. How much work there is in this world, ere nature becomes subdued to the use of man and the progress of humanity! and how much remains undone! We have lectures and conventions, speeches, and books written, to demonstrate woman's right to labor; but the truth is, half the women are overworked already,

while the other half are only for exhibition. They are highly educated, not for work, but for show; not for the art of doing, and doing with such skilled execution that all drudgery shall be taken out of labor, and woman's sphere be filled with those beneficent industries that train all the faculties into symmetrical grace and proportion. And so we read lately of a highly accomplished woman who had been educated here in the East, who starved to death because she could find nothing to do. Music and French and drawing were good in their way and in their sphere; but, when the strain and stress came, no faculty had been touched and trained to meet the conflicts of life. And so in a place where there was work all around, and woman's work too, that waited to be done, the highly educated girl could not do it; and lay down and starved and died. Indolence, and the love of languishing ease, had been overcome; but vanity had come in their place, and shaped the whole plan of study, and determined the whole style of character. Self in one shape had given way; and self in another and more specious form had succeeded. The kingdom within had changed one dynasty for another, while the foundations of character remained just the same, and just as frail and flimsy. And so, again, Tibni died, and Omri reigned.

4. And the same is true in a great many of those

changes of opinion, or conversions from one faith to another, which, when you sift them, are nothing more than the change of one form of self-opinion for another. Faith really progressive is always humble. Its enlarging view is like the ascent of an acclivity, giving at every step a wider horizon, and a purer air, above the clouds and the storms. But, in order to gain such a faith, one must always hold the attitude of a learner and a disciple. In the place of these, may come the pride of science, the conceit of opinion, or the dogmatism of sect. And a man may renounce the dogmas of superstition, and become a convert to the dogmas of infidelity, and be a greater bigot than ever, without any of that radical change of character which places his mind in sweet and humble attitude toward all the Divine revelations, whether from the spirit world or the natural. No matter what a man is converted from, or converted to, so long as he does not hold his opinions with the spirit of a child: it is one dynasty going out, and another coming, just as hard and despotic as the former. How many of these sudden conversions which we hear of, from one sect to another, are not progressions of faith, but revolutions of self-opinion!

So we find represented in these old scriptures those changes and revolutions in our inner world of thought and passion, which never make a man better, but only change the form of his own selfhood. There is no such revelation anywhere else, of the mysteries of human nature; and it even flashes forth through the proper names of the Old Testament, which become the labels of the passions that stir in human hearts everywhere. Every mind has some ruling love that gives unity and direction to all its powers. The ruling love changes sometimes through the whole of a man's life, taking one form in youth, another in manhood, and another still in age; one form in men, and another form in women. In youth, it may be love of pleasure; in manhood, love of glory; and, in age, love of ease: in women, it may be love of show; in men, love of money, — and all only self in variant shapes, with only the difference that one is a more handsome and successful imitation of goodness than another, but without any soul of goodness in it. Conversion to Christ puts the soul of goodness into all. Then business has a new aim, — Christian living and beneficence. Education has a new aim, — to fit men and women to do something for social progress, and for lifting the burdens of humanity. Female education has a new aim, — the truest and most substantial womanhood, for work and not for show; and young women need not wait for a political revolution before they begin an education, physical, moral, and intellectual, to fit them for the noble mission they are called to. I do not believe that there is any public opinion which bars woman from learning any thing or doing any thing in this world which she will do well; and, suppose there is, what has she to do but to disregard it, and revolutionize it, as the first success will be sure to do? Fealty to the Divine Master will give her the will and the power. And, the whole line of evil reigns once given up for the reign of Christ, there is no change of faith after that, but from glory to glory. Tibni dies, and all his line becomes extinct, that Christ may become all in all. No need of going from one sect to another, for that is only a change from one *human* master to another. The Christ involves and comprehends them all, and a great deal more besides; and change, with Him, is nearing the sun-bright summits which overlook all the fields of thought, and from which all the artificial lines of division fade away and disappear. When the reign of Christ comes in, and the reign of Ahab and all his line goes out, the end for which you live will be to do the work of Christ here on the earth, to leave the earth better than you found it. Education, all education, is for godly and beneficent living. Preparation for death is a preparation for larger and more angelic activities, with those who are more swift to do God's will; because the fetters of earth have broken away, and the reign of Christ supplants every form of self, and becomes all in all.

# PILATE.

John XVIII. 37: "Pilate therefore said unto him, Art thou a king, then? Jesus answered, Thou sayest that I am a king. To this end was I born, and for this cause came I into the world."

TO understand the whole scene of Jesus before Pilate, we must remember the state of mind in the Roman governor. He is at a loss what to do, and he hardly knows what he is saying. He echoes mechanically the word "truth," which had just fallen from the lips of Jesus. He is afraid of his prisoner; for the real character of Jesus beams out on his trial with commanding majesty. Jesus had said, "My kingdom is not of this world." — "Art thou a king, then?" says Pilate, disposed at first to a little banter and cavil. Then comes the reply, which has since been cited as the highest reach of the moral sublime, " Yes, I am a king" (so we should render). "To this end was I born, and for this cause came I into the world, that I should bear witness unto the truth. Every one who is of the truth heareth my voice." — "Truth," echoes Pilate timidly. "What is truth? I don't understand." And, shrinking both from an acquittal and from condemnation of Jesus, he went out to talk with the Jews privately, and persuade them of the innocence of Jesus.

I do not know of any character drawn so true to the life, with so few touches, as the character of Pilate in the narrative; and it proves irresistibly, with similar touches elsewhere, the authenticity of the fourth Gospel. Nobody could have imagined this. Observe the man and his difficulties. He is the Roman governor of Judæa, under Tiberius Cæsar. There are three parties whom he is anxious not to offend. The tyrant will recall him if there is trouble in his province which he cannot manage, when he must go back to Rome in disgrace. On the other hand, the Jews hate the Roman power, and, if not gratified, will chafe under it, and rebel. Both these two parties must be pleased. Then there is a third. He has some dregs of conscience in him yet; and he would like to do right, if he can without producing trouble and agitation. His wife has had a dream, warning him against participating in the death of Christ; and his superstitions are alarmed. So he trembles and vacillates between fear of the emperor, fear of the Jews, and fear of his own conscience within. He knows his prisoner is innocent, and that simple justice demands of him to pronounce acquittal from the judgment-seat. But this man claims to be a king. "Ah! they will be sending reports of me to Rome, that I have winked at treason; and there will be trouble there." He attempts various expedients. First, he tries to cajole these Jews, and persuade them to release Jesus. They refuse, and demand his life. Then Pilate tries to put the responsibility upon them. "Take him, and crucify him yourselves." They remind him that the Jewish tribunals have not the power of capital punishment. Jesus must be put to death, if at all, under Roman law, of which you, Pilate, are the magistrate. Then Pilate makes another shift. Herod of Galilee is at Jerusalem; and Pilate sends his prisoner to Herod, pretending that the case belongs to Herod's jurisdiction. Herod sends Him back. Then Pilate orders Christ to be scourged, thinking that by this the Jews will be satisfied, and sends Him out before them bleeding from the thongs, and says, "Only look upon the man." So far from being pacified, their rage kindles anew at the sight of blood; and "Crucify him!" goes up from the whole multitude. At last Pilate delivers up his prisoner to be crucified by his own soldiers, but orders water to be brought, and washes his hands before the people, saying, "I am innocent. See ye to it. His blood be upon you."

This is Pilate, eminently a representative man. We know something of him from profane history; but in this record he stands out with more amazing individuality. He personifies one of the types of human character, with indescribable naturalness, and is another name for vacillation and indecision. Let us take him now to represent this style of action; and, having seen where its weakness lies, let us pass on, and see how it may be cured, and how indecision may be turned into Christian strength and energy.

Four things will indicate the marks and symptoms of this infirmity of human nature, and show us when we are sliding into it.

1. The first is a disposition to put off our responsibilities upon others, and deny the jurisdiction of our own essential duties. And, when we wish to avoid a disagreeable duty, and try to put it upon Herod, we generally do it under pleas and pretences which are very specious, and which serve to flatter our self-love. Oh, our qualifications are not equal to it! Our experience is small, and some one else will do a great deal better than we can. Under this charming guise of amiability and modesty, we are complimenting, at the same time, our own humility, and the rare talent and ability of our friend over the way. Some persons pass through life shunning responsibilities which fairly belong to them, solely through that fear of man which bringeth a snare. And so there are vast powers which are never used, and vast energies which are never developed. Even in making up the judgments that belong to us, how liable are we to betake ourselves to the sheltering judgment of some

one else, in any case which involves censure and agitation. An emphatic yes or no from our own judgment-seat might settle at once and forever a question which otherwise is kept open for controversy and dissension, as the question is tossed to and fro between Herod and Pilate. Between a positive faith in Christianity, and a clean rejection thereof, we must find a middle ground, — between two wings a place that will offend neither; and we must shun all controversy, and keep the peace, not remembering that it is the positive and negative of the electric currents, which, coming together, forge the thunderbolts that shake the air.

2. The second expedient of this infirmity of human nature is compromise, or trying to get into some halfway house between right and wrong, between truth and falsehood. Some half-measure will probably satisfy both Tiberius and the people; and then our own consciences are soothed and drugged with the reflection that we have prevented a more terrible evil by choosing a less one. An overwhelming yes or no would have pushed things to extremes, whereas a negative positive will keep them on middle ground between the two. This has been tersely called, splitting the difference between God and the Devil; and when we do this, we do not consider that the latter power is mightily strengthened by the process, and emboldened mightily to ask more. Thus every com-

promise necessitates two more; and they increase in geometrical ratio, until the adversary has us completely under his feet. Half-measures with iniquity make it stronger. The scourging excites no compassion, but whets the appetite for blood till the cry of "Crucify!" rises with more unappeasable thirst for vengeance.

3. The third expedient of this infirmity of our nature is, to shift the blame upon others after the wrong is done. Acting from this state of mind, we never take any share of the guilt ourselves, for we think it all belongs to those bad people who made the excitement. The Pilates of all ages ward off their self-accusations by blaming their circumstances, never dreaming that it is the special duty and prerogative of human virtue to conquer circumstances, and change them. And to help on this expedient, and persuade ourselves of innocence, we are very apt to resort to religious rites and ceremonies. The Jewish law required, that when a murder had been committed, and the murderer was undiscovered, the elders of the city should wash their hands over an animal offered in sacrifice; saying, "Our hands have not shed this blood, neither have our eyes seen it. Lay not this innocent blood to thy people's charge." And then the guilt of the murder should not rest upon the city. Similar rites of purgation belonged to the Greek and Roman religions. It is the last

expedient employed to dim the consciousness of responsibility, to wash out the stains upon the conscience, not by repairing the wrong, but by the shows and mummeries of a pious ceremony. Guilt becomes the most hopeless and deep-seated, when it conceals itself under the hypocrisies of religious rites; and the conscience is then most effectually drugged and silenced.

4. The last thing which characterizes this infirmity of character is, that it falls with tenfold disaster into the very ruin it seeks to shun. Let us travel a little beyond the record, and see what became of this Roman magistrate, who sought a half-way house between right and wrong. He lost the confidence of all parties, and was called back to Rome in disgrace. Herod, who was made his friend that day, became his bitterest enemy. The dream of his wife, foreboding evil, was more than realized. The faint remnants of conscience, which appeared at the trial of Jesus, were soon extinguished; and Pilate became intolerably cruel. The Jews hated him, and accused him to the emperor; Herod hated him; the emperor hated him, and banished him to Gaul; he hated himself and his own life, and died miserably by his own hand. Such is the finish of the picture of this sleek Roman magistrate, who sought a half-way house between right and wrong, but perished without finding it.

Eighteen hundred years have passed away, and

Jesus is again before Pilate; and the same question comes up anew, Art thou a king, then? "Yes," says Jesus, "I am a king. I was born to be a king, and to this end came I into the world. Ye call me Master and Lord · and ye say well, for so I am." And yet we are now told there are two parties, both of which must be satisfied, and compromised with. One bows in acknowledgment of the immaculate purity and the authority of Jesus: the other party denies these; says He made mistakes, and was sinful, and was vindictive, and that the story of His life and miracles is myth and fable. Stripped of all soft and deceptive language, that is the issue between what are called the extremes of the Unitarian denomination; and we are told that we must find some middle way between these extremes, some split between a yes and a no on this plain question. "We must lean as flexibly as we can both ways,"—this is the language of the council of the National Conference,—"as flexibly as we can both ways, without losing our balance." I think that a denomination which undertakes the work of Pilate, "leaning flexibly both ways," will find the *doom* of Pilate, which is suicide. For, lift up your eyes, and see! He cometh in his kingdom; and his own words, "I am a king, and to this end was I born, and for this came I into the world," have still their daily fulfilment; for still He rules both the foremost thought and practice of the ages. And his church, more than ever conscious of his presence and inworking Divine energy, originates, leads on, and inspires all the advanced civilizations of the world, and the sweetest self-sacrifice in the cause of humanity. Is this an hour to stand and play the game of Pilate, when the words "*I am a king*" are having their fulfilment over the world and adown the centuries; when He comes to rule right royally over all this clear, earnest, and comprehensive faith, which, amid darkness and vacillation and doubt and uncertainty, opens the portals of immortality, shows both worlds in their organic relations with each other, and lights up the river of death with the splendors of an everlasting morning?

There is still another and more special and individual application. The subject, I think, rebukes all our half-professions in Christianity; all that halting discipleship which would make the gospel a compromise between Christ and the world, between religion and philosophy. He is indeed king to us, or He is nothing. He has no claim over us any more than Socrates or Seneca, nor so much as the philosophers of to-day, who have all the light of the new science and discovery; or else He has all claim over us, over faith and affection and life and practice, as that power of the Godhead which takes up our weak and lowly natures, creates them anew in his own image and likeness, and enriches them with the inbreathings and indwellings of the Holy Ghost. For it is either unwarranted assumption, or else it is tender invitation out of the depths of heaven,— the voice which comes to us even to-day, "All that the Father hath is mine;" "Come unto me, and I will give you rest." None that have come ever found those words deceptive or untrue; for it is rest from distraction and doubt, rest from weakness and vacillation, rest from the troublous uprisings of conscience, rest from debates whether there be any future life, or any God even, and repose on the bosom of his forgiving and cleansing love, within the peace and the sunshine of an eternal world.

# THE GOURD.

JONAH IV. 9: "Doest thou well to be angry for the gourd?"

PERHAPS no book has been the subject of so much banter and ridicule, among persons some of whom probably never studied or even read it, as the Book of Jonah. It is one of the minor prophets, not written by Jonah himself, but by some one who makes the name and history of the prophet the framework on which to hang some great clustering truths. It was written — so say the best critics — about four hundred years before Christ, and makes the traditional facts in the life of a prophet, who had lived, say a hundred years before, the basis of some important ethical doctrines addressed to the time and age. The form of it was just the one to be addressed to a Hebrew people of that age. The essence and spirit of it are beyond that age, and beyond this age as well. If you should ask me whether I believe the fact that stands out boldly in the body of the narrative — the swallowing of Jonah by a sea-monster, and the casting him up again — is to be believed, I should say for myself, I should never think of believing it, any more than I should think of believing as fact the frame and dress of "Pilgrim's Progress." It is of no consequence whether it were fact or not. I do not believe that Hamlet ever saw his father's ghost in just the way he describes the scene, nor that Macbeth ever saw Banquo's ghost with the long line of future kings, nor that Shakspeare believed he did. None the less do we receive the wonderful revelations of human nature found in those two tragedies. I do not suppose the narrative of the Prodigal Son is given to us in Luke as biography, or that Jesus cared whether we received it as such, or not. Of this Book of Jonah, however, two things are very obvious. There must have been an historical basis for it; and such a man must have lived and acted. The book is as full of human nature as it could well hold, and has such a human savor about it as gives it an air of intense reality. Then, again, the highest religious truths are so imbedded in the narrative, it is so packed with them we might say, that its allegorical character cannot be mistaken. The omnipresent voice of Divine rebuke that always follows us when we shirk our duty, or run away from the mission we are called to; the trouble that follows and involves us; the all-abounding Divine Mercy, free forgiveness on repentance and turning to the Lord; salvation even for the heathen on these conditions, a doctrine shocking to Jewish prejudice; the all-controlling and guiding

Providence that uses the individual for its great ends, the Providence of God in little things as well as great, in the withering of a plant not less than in the destruction of a city, anticipating our Saviour's doctrine of the sparrow's fall, — these are all conspicuous on the face of the narrative. They shine out clearly above the discoveries of that age, and above the theology even of this age.

But the personal history of the prophet himself is marvellously instructive. Jonah is emphatically and largely a representative man. There are two classes of troubles to which we are all subjected, and which sometimes have the very opposite influences on our tempers and lives. How often do you find that the small troubles are the hardest ones to bear! Yea, that our little griefs are the ones which bring the greatest amount of vexation and suffering. The great sorrows bring their own compensations and remedies: they melt us down into a sweet humility and tenderness, and bring us very near to the Lord. The smaller griefs have sometimes exactly the opposite results. They chafe and irritate, and drive us far away from the Divine refuge and love. What a burst of devotion came from the prophet when his great trouble overwhelmed him!

"I cried by reason of my distress to the Lord,
And he heard me.
Out of the depth of the underworld I cried,

And thou didst hear my voice.
Thou didst cast me into the deep, into the heart of the sea;
And the flood compassed me about.
All thy billows and thy waves passed over me;
And I said, I am cast out before thine eyes,
Yet I will look again to thy holy temple.
The waters compassed me about, even to the life;
The deep enclosed me round about;
Sea-weeds were bound around my head;
I sank down to the foundations of the mountains;
The bars of the earth were about me forever.
Thou hast brought up my life from the pit, O Lord my God!
When my soul fainted within me, I remembered the Lord;
And my prayer came to thee, to thy holy temple."

The whole description shows that the waves of a mighty trouble had broken over him, and that they woke the most fervid aspirations, and the most sublime and undoubting faith in God.

But now the scene changes: deliverance came; and our hero is sitting down on the eastern side of Nineveh, but in a frame of mind how vastly different! He is sick of life, and weary of the world. He wishes himself dead, and exclaims, "It is better for me to die than to live!" What is the matter now? Has the wave of some heavier calamity broken over him? Has he been plunged into depths of woe more terrible than the maw of the sea-monster that swallowed him up? Is it a more bitter calamity that now changes his strain of devotion to a wail of despair?

Oh, no! not that, *but his gourd has wilted.* It sprang up in a night; and he got under its shelter, and Jonah was exceedingly glad of the gourd. But a worm gnawed at the root of it, as worms are very apt to do, and so the gourd withered away; and now Jonah is without consolation. One would think it no great matter for him to change his position; but there he sits doggedly in the hot sun, and curses his fate. And the Lord said to him, " Doest thou well, to be angry for the gourd?" And he replied, " I do well to be angry, even unto death." And the curtain falls; and Jonah passes from our view forever, in this most uncomfortable and distressing frame of mind.

Even so. While we apply our religious theories to the greater sorrows, we are very apt to leave out the smaller ones, and lose all the good concealed in them. To endure small griefs well, and turn them to good account, is evidence, undoubtedly, of a more advanced spiritual culture, than is shown in enduring great griefs. It is quite as important to take these small griefs up into the economy of life, and discern their meaning, for the reason that the small ones beset us every day, whereas the great ones come but once or twice in a lifetime, and perhaps, when they do come, break open for us a way of entrance into the Divine love.

These small trials are of two kinds. There are some which come from within. They are produced by no external event whatsoever: not even the loss of the gourd can be put in as the cause of them; but a man's surroundings, of whatever kind, only excite and manifest them, and take on their shades and colorings. They are projections which some people make from their own souls, and which thence form the world they live in. Just as the soul which rays out warmth and sunshine will make all outward things take on its own irradiations; so the soul whose chronic state is dark and troublous, will surely ray out the darkness upon all things. Such an one will overlay with darkness the most blessed sunshine that ever fell on terrestrial objects, and make them reflect the hues of his own heart; whereas he whose soul flings out of itself the sunshine of a benevolent disposition will make it gild the darkest places with a heavenly light. So, then, in a most important sense, we create the world we live in every day. Its events and environments are simply the material which God furnishes; and out of ourselves comes the energy that makes them into hideous shapes and robes them in sombre hues, or else clothes them in the colors of a kindly heart and a heavenly mind. And hence the little troubles or the little mercies of the hour. Even if his gourd had not wilted, this peevish prophet would have rayed the trouble out of him, sitting there in sight of Nineveh, with its six hundred thousand inhabitants, angry with the Lord because he would not destroy the city, that he, Jonah, might have the honor of uttering a prediction. Just like the men who are always foreboding ruin and disaster, and who think, for that reason, that ruin and disaster are bound to come, and who are exceedingly disappointed unless these do come. Here, after all, was the seat of the trouble, and not the loss of the gourd.

However, these little griefs are not all of them pure creations from within. The minor troubles do beset us, sometimes coming into the house as unwelcome guests and there taking up their abode, sometimes springing upon us from coverts, unawares. They may be the very hardest to bear because we have no philosophy to apply to them. For great sorrows, we have the consolations of religion and the sympathy of friends. These others are too small for consolation and condolence. They do not crush into us like the great ones, but come drop, drop, with chafings and corrodings; and so we think we do well to be angry for the gourd.

But we do *not* well; and we are liable to three mistakes about them, which being once understood, we shall be able very thoroughly to disarm them.

Our first mistake is, that we think that there is a special Providence in the great troubles, but no Providence at all in the small ones. When destruction yawned to receive him, the prophet recognized the hand of God, and betook himself to prayer: "All thy billows have gone over me;" but when his gourd wilted, he took to cursing, evidently not supposing that God was in the small event just as much as in the greater. As if He who made the great sea-monster that roved in the deep waters, did not fashion just as much the little worm that ate into the roots of the vine that shaded the prophet's temples. So it is always. Great calamities are "ordered," we say; and so we are awe-struck and subdued, and submit with the best possible grace. And yet the small events are ordered in just the sense that the great ones are; since the great ones, when you analyze them, are nothing else than a congeries of ten thousand little ones; and it were absurd to say that God is in the whole, and not in all the little threads and fibres that make up the millionth part. Just as the Divine Omnipresence glows in the little violet which you tread under your feet, not less than in the troops of stars that whirl in mighty constellations through the rounds of space. so the Divine Providence is not less in small events than in great catastrophies. This being always acknowledged, you will no more be angry because the gourd has wilted, than you will be angry because there fell at your side the friend whom you composed with reverence and prayer to his everlasting rest.

But again: these Jonahs are very apt to make another mistake,—that of thinking they have more to bear than other people have, and that their annoyances are very peculiar. They think, very likely, that every path but their own is a path of roses. The worms that eat at the root of the gourd come most to *our* fields and gardens; the accidents of life break in upon *our* domestic arrangements, while the arrangements of others keep on without interruption; and those others lead a charmed life, and so keep their tempers sweet and cool, while ours are constantly pricked and fevered with the nettles and the thorns. But you would find, I think, if the domestic history of any family were unrolled to you, that each had its full share of these minor troubles; that they fall about equally over the surface of society, and are distributed somewhat on the principle of the rain. Sometimes there is more here, and less there; but the average quantity is about the same every year, and alike in one place, as another of the same latitude. So these infinitesimal griefs are distributed silent and unseen, as indispensable in the probation of man.

But we are liable to still another mistake. As with all other little things, we are very likely to undervalue them as tests of character, and as having a mighty and transforming power upon our whole inward being, and shaping the very soul itself to its high destiny. In the small trials, the action of the soul is perfectly free and spontaneous; and so its very flavor and quality are made manifest. It is not so in the great trials, when the mighty billows break over us, and we bend like an osier to the waves. In those great trials, there is one-half of our nature that is hushed and held in abeyance; and, under the Divine compassion, it might be like sailors in a storm, we repent of our sins, and bow down in prayer. How fervently the prophet prayed out of what he calls the bowels of hell! What else could he do? He must seek the Divine refuge then, for nothing else remained. It is quite otherwise when he sits at ease, and waits to see Nineveh destroyed. Then he acts himself; and his soul rays out of him without hinderance. In the great trials, the Lord bends us, and holds us in his hand. In the little ones, we spring back to our normal condition; and so we put our very selves into these, and fill them out with just what we are. See, then, how vastly important is their place in the great school of Providence, that trains us for immortality. The little trials are, in fact, the only real ones; for those do try us, and test our quality, and show to what extent our regeneration is advancing. When rent by ghastly wounds, we lie submissive and bleeding. When pricked by thorns, our spirit rays out of us its own fragrance; and when the very spirit of Christ — gentleness, goodness, and long-suffering — flows out spontaneously into the smaller trials, and makes them fragrant with the breath of heaven, then only are we ripening for the heavenly abodes. See their place, then, in the school of probation we are going through, and how constantly and surely they are passing judgment on our inward state and qualities.

In truth, we are not fit for any great trial or emergency until we have first learned to pass through the smaller ones with serenity and meekness, any more than a child is fit for the higher schools until he first learns the rudiments and the alphabet. The smaller trials of every day are the primary schools of Providence; and out of these, if at all, we pass to the higher ones, and take up the sublimer and more triumphal strains, "I am persuaded, that neither death nor life, nor the principalities and powers of angels, nor things present, nor things to come, nor height, nor depth, nor any power in the whole creation, shall be able to separate us from the love of God, which is in Christ Jesus our Lord."

# SPIRITUAL RESURRECTION.

JOHN V. 25 : "Verily I say unto you, the hour is coming, and now is, when the dead shall hear the voice of the Son of God: and they that hear shall live."

IT was a scene of desolation and death. Jesus looked around him, and saw among the Jewish people only a dead formalism, and among the Gentile people only stolid ignorance of all spiritual things. There was the droning of the synagogues, but the worship had become dead, — worship in which there was very little knowledge of God, or love of men; and outside the synagogues were the heathen population, among whom belief in their own gods had ceased to be operative. It is in reference to this state of things that Jesus says to the Jews, "The time is coming, and now is, when the dead shall hear the voice of the Son of God: and they that shall listen to it shall live."

The words very soon were fulfilled. Jesus departs from Judæa into Galilee. He leaves Jerusalem, where his message was rejected, and in Galilee organizes his two bands of disciples, the twelve and the seventy; and they go out and preach. It was not many months before all Galilee was shaken from sleep. Jesus says, when they bring back reports of their mission, "I see Satan as lightning falling from heaven. I see his power going out like a meteor trailing down the sky." The revolution which began in Galilee rolled up to Jerusalem; and the powers there saw that they must go down under it, unless they could put the Author of it out of the way. They did put Him out of the way; and they brought Him more directly into the way again; for He came to his church and his people from the spiritual side in the power of his resurrection.

It is the moral resurrection which is described in the text: waking out of spiritual torpor and death at the voice of the Son of God. The words of the text, however, had their fulfilment, not alone at that hour, and there in Palestine, but ever since, when men listen to the voice of the Son of God. But what is this spiritual awakening, this new consciousness in human nature, produced by the voice of Christ, when they that listen do live? *The resurrection from death unto life through the voice of the Christ in the human soul,*—let us make this the theme of discourse this Easter morning.

"*Spiritual death,*" "sleeping in the dust," "dead in sin," "lying in the grave," all this phraseology is used in the New Testament to describe a state of religious indifference and insensibility. It is want of thought, want of interest, want of care or attention towards the great questions that appeal to man as a spiritual being. The indifference may not be uniform and unbroken; but with many persons it prevails at last, and quenches all earnest faith and all deep and fervid sensibility. The most confirmed unbeliever is not uniformly indifferent. He may have only postponed the question for a convenient season, that never comes. There are times when a light from above flashes down among his faculties, and startles him with a glimpse of the mysterious grandeur of his being. "What went before me, and what will follow," says one of these men, "I regard as two black, impenetrable curtains which hang down at the extremities of human life, and which no living man has yet drawn aside. Behind the curtain of futurity a deep silence reigns. None who have once penetrated the veil will answer those they have left behind. All you can hear is a hollow echo of your question, as if you shouted into a chasm." And having shouted into the chasm, and got no answer, he concludes no answer is to be had; and so buries himself deeper, and sleeps sounder than ever, in his spiritual grave. But let us come more directly to the signs and indications of spiritual death.

I call that a state of spiritual death where there is no earnest inquiry in regard to fundamental truth, where there is no time set apart for the subject, where it is never approached with the brooding spirit of thought. This indifference often takes the form of a false liberality, or an affected contempt for disputes and controversies about religion. Its language sometimes is, "I am sick of hearing about doctrines concerning which nobody agrees. Let them have the whole dispute to themselves. I stand aloof. I care nothing about it. I mind my own business, being quite sure that there can't be much good in that which is the subject of so much division and disagreement." If the point of the objection were, that we ought not to approach in a wrong temper of mind a subject of so much consequence, it were all well. But more than this is implied in this train of remark. It is an aversion to the whole subject of gospel truth, an unwillingness to enter in earnest upon its lessons. And what a position is this for a rational and immortal mind to hold and defend! God is seeking to come to us, and find us, and enrich us with Himself. His word and his works copy out his eternal mind, and show forth his purposes, and proclaim his perfect will. It is against these that such a person closes his eyes or turns away, and says, "I care nothing about it." Well do the Scriptures compare this indifference to sleep in the grave. The man who sleeps is, for the time being, dead to all the magnificence about him. The light of the morning is pouring through his windows, the earth is rejoicing as if created anew, and a thousand objects have put on afresh their garments of beauty and brightness. But all this is lost upon the man who sleeps: his mind is a blank, or he converses only with phantoms; he is insensible as the clods beneath him to all the glowing scenery that opens above and around him. It is just so with those who are spiritually asleep. There is a world of spiritual light against which their eyes are closed; there is a system of truth which explains the mysteries of our lowly condition; there is a Christianity which sheds a Divine radiance over all our affairs, and opens a world within us and a world beyond, revealing its objects in colors of heavenly brightness. And all this has no existence to those that are asleep, who will not inquire and learn, and come to the truth as it is in Jesus. Maintain, if you will, this indifference, but know also that the morning hath strewn the earth with light, and that skies you never look upon are bending over you.

Again: that is religious indifference where one makes no inquiries about himself, the condition of his own mind and heart, how he stands affected toward God, and whether or not he is prepared to meet Him in judgment. He should not only ask what is true, but he should ask specifically what are the conditions of his salvation, and whether or not he has complied with them. He is asleep, he is dead, who has not revolved this question with all that solicitude and care which its importance demands. For we stand affected toward God, and toward his universe, and toward eternity, by the state of mind and heart within us; for here are the causes that create for every man a paradise or a hell. "What shall it profit a man if he gain the whole world, and lose his own soul?" Undoubtedly the question crosses everybody's mind, more or less. "What am I, and what shall I become?" But with the man not perseveringly insensible, it will be more than a casual inquiry. He will often retire into himself; he will come with a silent and reverent mind to his Bible, and give himself thoroughly to the work of examination. He will know whether or not he can "read his title clear;" and he will revolve the question with the charter of his salvation open before him. Who are those men who come with ripe experience, with heaven-lifted eyes, with trust which the world cannot shake, and with a piety which the world cannot chill? Did they sleep themselves into such a state of mind? No. They come from watchings and private communings, which sometimes, even at midnight, have "chased repose from their eyelids." They are those who have retired often from the strife of men and the conflicts of business, and sent home questionings of themselves. And often have they found, that when with the world, they felt satisfied with themselves, yet when retired, and looking into their hearts, the sins of years would "stream o'er their memories like a flame;" and, when holding to their minds the mirror of God's word, gleams of eternity, not less vivid, would reveal them to themselves. These are the hours when the answer to the question, "What shall I do to be saved?" comes at length distinct and definite, and when the problem of destiny is solved. However much of stir and of noise one may make in the world, yet he is asleep in its dust, he is insensible to those things which are of eternal importance to himself, unless he comes earnestly to this business of self-examination.

Again: I call that a state of spiritual death, where there is no confession of the religion of Christ, no combination and effort to extend its sway. Any one who has had a living experience of the hope, the peace, the renovation, which comes of religious faith, will hear ever the call within him to impart it. Hence the church of Christ, if the Christ live within it, is by necessity a missionary society. It is a force in the world, to redeem the world and save it; and, where the Christ is truly received, He gathers his followers around Him as their living Head, and fulfils his promise with them, "Lo, I am with you alway," and through this new organism goes forth to serve the world. "Where two or three are gathered in my name," is the promise, "there am I in the midst of them." Where they do not gather in his name, and do his work, his life dies out of them, if they ever had it. "For if a man abide not in me, he is a branch cut off, and he withers and dies."

Such are the symptoms of what Jesus calls the spiritually dead; and what is the resurrection out of this state, which He describes? Answer: It is a new consciousness of life; and its first token is a new consciousness of the truth of the soul. Spiritually dead men do not really know that they have souls. They really regard themselves as a more intelligent race of animals, who live and die only a more rational animal life and death. Yea, the scientists to-day are debating the question, whether any thing more is to be made of a man than that. The first boon which the gospel brings is an intense and vivid consciousness of the value of the soul,—a value so great that it flings dimness over all other values; so that if a man gain the whole world, and lose the soul, he suffers an infinite loss. It is not merely the fact of immortality that gives this consciousness. No: the first operation of the Holy Spirit within you, will make you conscious of an untold capacity, both for suffering and joy,—a suffering and a joy compared with which the pains and pleasures of the body are contemptible indeed. Said a man once who had perverted, neglected, and abused his spiritual nature, and drowned the conscience out of it, but, waking up too late to a consciousness of its tremendous reality, "This body is all weakness and pain ; but my soul, as if stung by torment to greater strength and spirit, is full powerful to reason, and full mighty to suffer; and that which triumphs within the jaws of immortality is doubtless immortal;" and as for a Deity, " Nothing less than an Almighty could inflict what I feel." And such is the twofold resurrection of all who are in the graves of spiritual death, who come forth at the voice of the Son of God. " They that have done good to the resurrection of life, and they that have done evil to the resurrection of condemnation." The soul waked up to a vivid consciousness of its own power, neither enjoys nor suffers like an animal. There is an angel tone to its song of victory, and something more than mortal mingles in the voice of its wail. But another and decisive token of the resurrection from spiritual death is the Christ of consciousness, — in Paul's language, the Christ formed within, as the hope of glory. " I in them," says Jesus, "and thou in me, that they may be made perfect in one, and that the world may believe that thou didst send me." It is the faith in Christ, and the love of Christ, growing more full and abounding, till his spirit is your spirit, his life your life, his filial love and tenderness entering into you and giving you a heart of flesh beating warm and full, and throwing off the old spiritual death robes. It is both a new heart and a new mind. If you have this, you will love his service, and love his work, and love his church, and bring into it souls consecrated to Him; for if any man be in Christ, he is a new creature. "Old things have passed away. Behold all things have become new." Such is death, and such is resurrection, — the only death that is to be feared, and the resurrection to everlasting life.

Bear with me in a word of exhortation and application of this subject. What avail these blessed Easter mornings if they find you in the graves of spiritual death? Has the Christian gospel, which is "the word of the Son of man," ever awakened you to a vivid consciousness of the real value of the souls that throb within you? Do you know their untold capacities for joy and for suffering? Do you know the grandeur and the tremendous possibilities of your own immortal natures? If so, I wonder you do not seem to be more alive to the reality. Has Jesus Christ ever dawned upon you, not as a man who died in Palestine eighteen hundred years ago, and whom you have done with, but as the Risen and the Glorified, the God with us, the Head of his church, who calls to you out of the bending heavens, and calls you to a consecration to Him and his service? Rise! Oh, rise with Him out of these graves of religious indifference and insensibility! Gather round Him as your living Head; and then you will share in the glory of his resurrection; for touched by Him, and made sharers of his spirit, his love, and his work, your souls within will become conscious of an inheritance and a joy, compared with which these earthly riches are as dross to the imperishable gold.

# CONVERSION.

———✦———

Acts XXVI. 19: "I was not disobedient unto the heavenly vision."

THE conversion of Saul of Tarsus is one of the most prominent facts in the Christian history; and it belongs to that section of Christian history which has never been called in question. There are four Epistles of Saint Paul which the most searching and captious criticism accepts as genuine; and in these the conversion of Saul of Tarsus is described in all its graphic details. It was only about twenty years after the death and ascension of Christ; and even if the Gospel histories had not come down to us, the experience and the work of Saint Paul fling back a light over the whole ground, and show its necessity as the basis of what follows. The sceptical criticism tries to account for Saul's conversion by the supposition, that he had fits or swoons, and saw only the spectres of his own mind. If so, it is the first instance in which fits and swoons have resulted in such enlargement of intellectual power as to mould the thought of the world for eighteen centuries.

But for other reasons the conversion of Saul of

Tarsus is a subject of exceeding interest. It illustrates the nature of *all conversion*, and the power of Christianity in producing it.

The city of Damascus is about six days' journey from Jerusalem. It stands on a green oasis amid a vast desert of sand, watered by crooning brooks, and embowered by delicious shade. Here was a synagogue of the Jews; and some of its members had been converted to Christianity. Saul comes from Jerusalem, armed with letters from the Sanhedrim, to bring the apostates to punishment. There is something in his errand uncommonly cruel, even for a Jew; for not only men, but helpless women, are to be dragged forth, and stoned to death. He is near the end of his journey; and Damascus, gleaming through its palm-trees, is already in sight. He is attended with a band of police-officers to help him in his work. The sun glares hot upon the sands; and you will see how much is meant when we are told that a brightness greater than the Syrian noon now surrounds these travellers, and overpowers them. You will notice the difference in the impressions made on the senses of the travellers. We have three different narratives of the event, which seem at first to disagree in minor details, though the disagreement disappears on critical examination. They all witness a light so sudden and intense that it blots out the Syrian day. The blaze of a greater light involves them. They cannot bear it, and fall upon their faces. They all hear a sound; but only to Saul there is a form within the light, and words within the sound, — Hebrew words, in which his own name is articulated aloud, "Saul! Saul! why persecutest thou me? It is hard for thee to kick against the goads. As vainly as the ox resists the sharp irons which drive him, so vainly do you resist my power that takes hold of you, and turns you. Go into the city, and it shall be told you what to do."

He tries to go, but he is in midnight darkness. The rest see again, but to Saul the green city is blotted out. He started from Jerusalem, the fierce spirit of the enterprise, breathing threatening and slaughter. He enters Damascus, where they lead him among the purling brooks, helpless as a child; and he is lodged in charity at the house of one of those Christians he came to persecute. Such is what is generally known as the conversion of Saul of Tarsus; but we have not yet come to the conversion itself. We must not suppose, from the garb of marvel in which it comes down to us, that the conversion itself was exceptional or anomalous. No genuine conversion ever suspends the laws of the mind, else why was this man selected from among others? and why was not the whole Jewish nation converted in a mass to Christianity? We lay off what is only special and adventitious; and then we shall see, in what remains, what all Christian conversion must be.

1. The peculiarity in the case of Saul was the open vision of the Lord Jesus Christ. This, however, was not necessary to his conversion to Christianity, and had no necessary connection with it. It was because this man was to be, not only a Christian, but an apostle. To be an apostle, it was necessary that he should see the Lord. To be an apostle, the disciple must not only have seen his Lord in the flesh, but must see Him after his resurrection. For the apostles were to be witnesses of that fundamental fact of Christianity. They were not only to preach Christ, but immortality brought to light, not through the reasonings of philosophy, but through the open demonstrations of the spirit-world. Hence the language of Christ, "I have appeared unto thee for this purpose, — to make thee a witness of those things which thou hast seen." And ever afterwards, when he speaks of his commission as an apostle, he appeals to the fact that he has seen the Lord Jesus. It is not logic, but *testimony*, and testimony to *things revealed;* revealed not to our groping senses, but in a light so broad and intense as to eclipse the sun of noonday. The other apostles make the same appeal the ground of their mission. "This same Jesus," as said Peter amid the Pentecostal scene, "hath God raised up, whereof we are all *witnesses*." Paul proba-

bly had never seen Christ in the flesh: but he is now at Jerusalem, only twenty years after the death of Christ, when the blood of his martyrdom was still fresh upon Calvary, and all the events of his wondrous ministry were fresh upon the tongues of men; so that the testimony and apostleship of this man alone, all other history aside, bring those great events before us, almost as the things of yesterday.

2. We must look afterward to find the genuine conversion of Saul to Christianity. For three whole years after this remarkable vision he disappears from history. He appears neither at Jerusalem nor at Damascus, but retires into Arabia. What his experience and employment there were he has not told us; but we are not left in doubt from the nature of the case. There he gives his remarkable powers to the investigation of this new system of faith; there all his Jewish learning comes into play; there are searched the old prophecies which converge in lines of light to the day of fulfilment; there the message of the risen Christ is pondered; there Paul's large discourse of reason brings the new faith to the test of examination; there new communings are had with the risen Christ; and there the Holy Spirit comes, with its subduing and transforming power.

There is in all genuine religious experience a secret province of the soul which cannot be laid open to the common gaze. The reticence of the apostle respecting those three remarkable years, we can well understand. It is only when he comes out of this retirement, and re-appears at Jerusalem, that we find the wonderful change. He left it, a hard, persecuting bigot, breathing threatening and slaughter. He re-appears, with a heart brimming over with love for all mankind, and writes that chapter on charity, which has been its sweetest lyric to all times and ages. He was a man not to be overpowered by visions, nor to surrender blindly his own reason and conscience, else he could not have been the masterly logician we find him afterwards. He pauses, reasons, examines, and prays. He takes three years for all this. And, out of this profound experience, he sets forth to others this same Christianity, with a self-devotion so entire, and a logic whose links are so warm with the Holy Ghost, that the theology of the Church has been largely run in its moulds.

3. Lay off, then, the garb of miracle and prodigy, and we come to that experience of the apostle, which shows what all Christian conversion must be. It is meeting the Christ somewhere on the journey of life, in a light above the mere light of nature, demanding our obedience. It is the Divine Law laid supremely on the conscience, and enforced with the sanctions of immortality. It may not be on the hot desert of life: it comes sometimes with the first dawnings of infant reason, a sweetly-beaming star that grows

to the splendors of the Syrian noon. Those who are turned thus early to a Christian life do not date their conversion from one marked and decisive epoch. Even with them, however, the process is just the same. The decisive choice is made, and made so early, that the will is bent by gentle and easy tractations to the Divine Will. The light from heaven *may* meet us later, for the first time, and on the sandy deserts of sin and unbelief. Then it becomes a landmark in our history, standing out bold and palpable; and all our after-life dates from it. But the nature of the change is ever the same. It is not a mere crisis of feeling and emotion: it is a change in the grand purpose of life. It is a choice to live no longer for ends that are narrow and selfish, but for ends that are broad, Christian, and humane. The heavenly vision breaks upon us, and the voice out of it is clear and commanding, and our response to it is strong and decisive, "Lord! what wilt thou have me to do?" It is the same law of Christ coming not audibly, but not less surely, not out of the sky, but through the heart, with a stillness like the summer breeze. You hear it in calls and pleadings to a Christian life; you hear it in the whole message of the gospel; you hear it from the pages of his Word, where the Spirit of Christ breathes through the letter, and says, "Come unto me." The open vision vouchsafed to Paul, only revealed the agencies that ever work within us, their voices breaking not upon the ear, but upon the reason and the conscience, because there they speak to our higher and nobler nature, and win us, not through the senses, but through the deepest convictions of the soul. Such is the nature of conversion as here revealed. Its results upon the life and character are not less manifest. Old things pass away, and all things become new. The hardness, the hate, the cruelty, the evil passions, the Pharisaic pride and bigotry, which made up the Saul of Tarsus, and which are latent or manifest in every natural mind,— all these melt down and are purged away, as the Christ of consciousness becomes full and abounding. But we are not to imagine that all this takes place through some sacred magic, or some irresistible grace. If Paul required three years of prayer and self-discipline and self-application before he took up the message of the new life, let us not imagine that we are to be exempt from the same conditions. These conditions observed, the changes wrought in the character are ever the same to every Christian believer,— the Christ coming, not through the sky, but melting into the soul, our Life, our Light, our Righteousness; transfusing those tender and humane sentiments that form the Christian atmosphere we breathe; resting on our souls as a new and incumbent Law; giving us an experience of the Divine

Love such as Jew or Pagan never had; giving us the evidence of a Life working within our life; giving us foretastes of heaven, and foresplendors of immortality.

Two points of special interest present themselves from this subject. One has respect to the dealings of God with his children. How tender is the Divine reserve! He never comes to us so as to break us down into machines, but always has respect to the prerogatives of our spiritual nature. He comes not to overwhelm from without, but to inspire from within, through self-convictions made deep and clear. God is here, but veiled. Christ is here, but veiled. If they broke upon us with a light that blotted out the sun, we should need, all the same, our days and years of thought, of prayer, of self-examination, of clear reason in the interpretation of the outward phenomena to make sure that it was no imposition on our wildering senses. These outward phenomena alone convert no one. Otherwise they would be given. Otherwise not an unconverted Jew would have remained in Jerusalem, and not an unconverted man would be living to-day.

But because of this Divine reserve in the manifestations from without, our listening to the voice within should be the more earnest and profound. For *there* come the revealings, which we disobey with tenfold danger. Out of them comes the voice which speaks with a more commanding, because a more interior authority; and happy is he who can say when it comes to him, "I was not disobedient to the heavenly vision."

# SELF-CONSECRATION.

MARK X. 21: "One thing thou lackest."

HAVE you never observed that character may be perfectly blameless, without any spots or blemishes to which the most fastidious could point the finger, and yet you feel that it lacks the crowning grace of manhood and womanhood? Do you not feel, even, that if put to the test, it would be found specious and illusive, and fail totally in the day of trial? It is well worth our most careful analysis to ascertain how even Christian accomplishment and religious culture may be only an appearance, and not a reality, very sure to subside and come to nothing when God makes up his jewels. The narrative from which I take the text describes a young man, who, deeply impressed with the wonderful works of Jesus, and convinced, evidently, of his Divine mission, comes to Him with the expectation of being his follower, and sharing the reward of his kingdom. Let us for a moment bring out this young man's characteristics, and see what was the thing which he wanted, to give substance and vitality to the whole.

1. His morality is perfect: here he stands the test where most people would have found rents and stains upon their garments. There is no more perfect morality anywhere than that described in the two tables of the Decalogue. Its requirements are lofty and pure, in striking contrast, not only with the abominations of heathenism, but with the human codes of all ages. We can point back even now to these ten voices from Sinai, as evidence that Judaism had something in it which was not a human development, but a revelation out of heaven, — a sphere of Divine Light come down amid the darkness. All these the young man has kept from his youth up.

2. Again: his religion is perfect so far as religion consists in observances and ceremonials; for there never was any worship more complete and punctilious in all its forms than the Jewish. Its stated gifts and offerings were perfect representatives and symbols, Divinely appointed and arranged, involving all periods of life, from childhood up to age. These, also, the young man had observed from his youth up.

3. Nor is this all. In personal graces and endowments he is also distinguished. They appear in his whole behavior, they bloom in all his manners. He comes to Jesus, and comes kneeling, with that graceful deference painfully lacking where the spirit of reverence has decayed. So sweet and lovable is

his deportment, that the Saviour is touched by it, and pauses to look at the young man. "Beholding," says the narrative, "He loved him." In these three things — an untainted morality, conformity to a national religion Divinely instituted, and in personal gifts and graces — he is rich, and in need of nothing. What was lacking? *Self-renunciation!* That word describes the whole thing which was wanting, and which being absent, all those other acquirements were only on the surface, and lacked a vital element within.

But what is this self-renunciation? Let us enter into its meaning more fully. It lies at the very threshold of a true life, which without it has not yet begun to be Christian; and I wish, in this sermon, to address more directly my young hearers, to whom I think the call to self-consecration comes with special earnestness. First we will see what is implied and involved in self-renunciation; then what are the mistakes respecting it which we ought to avoid.

1. Every person at some time, consciously or not, comes to a decisive choice between self and God. He comes into the free, conscious possession of the most precious gifts of mind and heart and soul and golden opportunity. He will use them in one of two ways. He will use them for objects mainly personal, in which case his end will be supremely within himself; and self-seeking and self-indulgence

will be the chief aim of his life. Even his moralities, his worship, and his charities will have only self at the heart of them; for they will be the decorations of his self-love, the gratifications of his vanity and pride. Or, on the other hand, these gifts of mind and heart and opportunity may all be held as God's, and not ours,— trusts committed to us, whereby to serve Him, and fill the sphere He has placed us in, with beneficence and blessing. When these gifts are consecrated to God's service, the Christian life has begun, and not till then: hence the sharp contrasts which the gospel presents to us, "He that is not with me is against me; and he that gathereth not with me scattereth abroad." This describes in full the distinction between Christ and the world, — being conformed to the world, or being transformed by the renewing of our minds. We have been accustomed to dwell upon the intrinsic worth and capacities of a human soul; and there is no exaggeration here, for it is out of such souls as are in you that God makes his highest angels. But the worth of the soul is only found when the soul is directed to right ends, and follows them with earnestness and singleness of purpose. If not so directed, and that early, you have only to look about you, and see how all its worth may be sacrificed and lost. Oh, the multitudes of men and women who began life with minds and hearts as fresh as yours, but whose souls dwindled and dried up until you would not know, except that they wear the human form, whether they were immortal beings or no! You need not send your imagination on into the future state in order to understand what is meant by gaining the world, and losing the soul. To lose the soul, is to have its powers, once waking into life with all the dew of the morning upon them, narrowed down towards nothing, and shrunken and shrivelled up like a scroll, in the pursuit of narrow and ignoble ends. To save the soul, is to have its powers heaven-directed and baptized into some work of life paramount to all personal comfort and ease and pleasure; to have them merged in the cause of Christ, which is the cause of human society and progress and regeneration. I have come to regard it as one of the beneficent arrangements of Divine Providence, that so many persons die young, and are thereby saved from that danger of collapse and deterioration which always attends unused or misdirected faculties here on the earth. But this loss of the soul is not necessary; and early self-consecration is the very thing that will save it. The difference between a consecrated and an unconsecrated life may not be obvious to you at the start; but their lines diverge wider and wider asunder, till the space between measures all the difference between heaven and hell.

The subsequent history of the young ruler has not been given to us; but we know just as well what it was, for we have seen it repeated again and again. Following him along into manhood and age, we should find him, in religion probably a Pharisee, whose inner life had oozed out upon the surface, and there hardened into a dry crust of conformity; in morality, a Jew, clutching his great possessions more desperately, strictly observing his legal righteousness, without any throbs of humanity and mercy beating through it; the bloom of youthful amiability gone, as belonging only to the surface of the man. Such manhood becomes when the soul is lost out of it, and only the semblance and the shell of it is left.

An unconsecrated womanhood goes down on the same line of deterioration. Its spiritual life does not grow richer and deeper, but the want of moral aim is attended with total want of moral earnestness; and a want of moral earnestness makes the character superficial and frivolous and worldly, and makes all accomplishments and acquirements mere devices to gain the admiration of society; and when their day is past, the heart is left unsatisfied and desolate and cold. The gifts of mind and heart unused, or used only for private ends, always diminish, leaving only the semblance of humanity, without its divine inspirations and rewards. It is not so with a consecrated life, which grows rich and full as its satisfactions increase. Then, for the first time, you know that God is with you, and that you are in the currents of his Providence. Then, for the first time, prayer is really answered; for we never pray with true faith, till we know we are working with God, and striving for the same ends that He has. Then your life is hid with Christ in God. Acting only within the circle of private aims and interests, you must always halt and calculate. You have always something to gain or lose, in ease, or comfort, or estate, or reputation; and you never come into that clear and single-eyed activity that unlocks all the faculties, and gives them easy and healthful play, until you have given them to the Lord. Hence, so much talent that is never used. Hence, too, the fact, that, when one has passed through this stage of self-renunciation, he learns for the first time the angel powers that slumbered within him. Then the arm is nerved, and the heart is strong. Acting only in the eye of man, and calculating personal consequences, you hesitate, and take to ciphering to see how it will pay. Acting only in God's eye, and cast upon Him without any reserve, all artificial limitation and halting leave you in the liberty wherewith Christ has made you free. We never come into complete possession of ourselves till we have first renounced ourselves, and live alone for Christ, or the work which He gives us to do. Hence the prime purpose for which the Church of Christ exists here upon the earth. It is to draw into it, and organize and consecrate to his work, all human souls that will be acceptive of his grace and love, that in them and through them He may come in his kingdom, and make earth to blossom anew. But you will ask, perhaps, my young hearers, why not wait a while, and begin the Christian life by and by, when we shall have more need of its consolations, and understand more about it. Answer. For a great many reasons, but for one which is prominent and decisive; and it is this. By waiting and delaying, you lose a golden opportunity that never will come round again. Only one period of youth is given to us; and it is more decisive and plastic over our whole future being than any other period can possibly be. A life consecrated at the beginning secures to itself a whole treasury of impressions and affections warmed and sanctified by the Holy Spirit, which become more central and abiding than those of any other period of life. They go down deeper into our natures then, because our natures are more susceptible and tender to receive them and hold them than they ever will be again. Persons, it is true, sometimes become converted later in life; but they are very apt to bring elements of character then which are flinty and earthly, and which even the fire of God's Spirit never melts out of them in this world, if it does in the world to come. It is to an early self-consecration, that our Saviour promises the guardian angels that always behold the face of the Father.

2. But do not mistake. When I say consecration to Christ, I mean the whole Christ, not anybody's poor human theories about Him. I mean the Christ of the New Testament, of his own Church Catholic, walking in the midst of the golden candlesticks, melting through the ages with greater and greater power and glory; not the Christ of some sect who have embalmed his dead body, and keep it laid away in the sepulchres of a past theology, calling that the Christ of to-day.

The difference between joining the Church of Christ and joining a sect, is this. The church, truly Christian and Catholic, will gather you around Him with no priest between, in the full belief that no human creed can contain Him, that none of our little formularies exhaust Him; but that your faith in Him is to grow larger and brighter as long as you live, and that your experience of his grace and love will grow more rich and tender to the last. The sect assumes that our first conception of Him shall be fixed and final; nay, that we shall go back and take the interpretation of a dark age, five hundred years ago, and embrace its skeletons as the Christ of to-day. Do not come to Him in this way. Come to Him without any priestly mediation, and enter into the freedom of his truth and love; and then you are consecrated to a Christian life, whose flowing on shall be a continuous progress in time and eternity.

Come to Him, then, that all your aims may be elevated, and made generous and pure. Come, that on the beatings of his heart your own love may be made larger and warmer and deeper. Come to Him as the perfect offering ; and as you pray, " O Lamb of God, my sacrifice," seek at his feet for a self-renunciation as complete as his. Come, that your faith in God whom He reveals may be always clear, and your faith in his children may be full of hope and confidence. Come, not to get into heaven, but that heaven may get into you, in its spirit of humility and never-failing charity. For, believe me, unless heaven first comes within, breathed through all the interiors of your minds, you shall find, when these bodies crumble about you, there is an awful gulf between heaven and you; but, if here you are one with Jesus in heart and purpose and life, you will then be ready with the elders about the throne, not for barren praises, nor selfish delights, but for larger and more holy activities in the kingdom of universal love. And then you will look back to the early time when you heard and obeyed the call of the spirit within to give yourselves to Christ without reserve, as the hour when the heavens did bend around you with their selectest influence, and their angels watched you with a thrill of joy, that a new soul had been won to their abodes.

"In childhood's spring, — ah, blessed spring!
    As flowers closed up at even
Unfold in morning's earliest beam,
    The heart unfolds to heaven.
Ah, blessed child, that trustingly
    Adores and loves and fears,
And to a Father's voice replies,
    'Speak, Lord: thy servant hears.'"

# CONDITIONS OF SPIRITUAL PROGRESS.

PSALMS LXXXI. 10: "Open thy mouth, and I will fill it."

THE figure of speech here used by the Psalmist, is that of a mother feeding her child. The sole condition on the part of the child is to receive what is given. Nothing great, nothing difficult, is required. No straining and reaching forth, but simply opening the mouth to be fed, as a condition of health and growth, and becoming strong. And the figure is exceedingly suggestive as to the conditions of our spiritual progress, — conditions which I think we are very apt to make too complicated and hard.

A distinction which Unitarians have been prone to overlook, or confound altogether, I propose, in this sermon, to bring out in as clear illustration as I can, and then apply it to the whole subject of spiritual growth and progress. It is the distinction between the *capacities*, the receptivities, of human nature, and its inhering and independent force. By its capacities, we mean its susceptibilities to receive what is given, like the child's capacity to receive food when hungry, or drink when thirsty, and thereby to thrive and grow. By its original force, we mean its intrinsic powers, self-contained and self-moving; making progress, not so much by food received from without, or from above, as by springs of action within. By asserting and dwelling largely on these original powers and attributes, Dr. Channing unfolded his views of the dignity of human nature, — views which tone and color his whole argument in that excellent volume lately published, entitled "The Perfect Life." I do not wish, by any means, to controvert the argument. It needed at the time to be set forth strongly and clearly. But I do think, that, when we dwell too exclusively on the intrinsic force and dignity of human nature, we waft perfume to its pride, and for real spiritual life and progress we substitute our swollen conceit and vanity; yea, more, we make spiritual progress a mighty difficult and uphill business. It is working our way to heaven, and working hard. It is trying to warm ourselves only by fires of our own kindling. It is trying to move by self-development, which is very much as if a man should try to lift himself. How many people tried this process of spiritual culture till they got discouraged, and gave it up, and then went over to Rome, or over somewhere else, where there was nothing to do but just make believe, and be saved!

"Open thy mouth, and I will fill it." The capacity of the soul, its receptivity, in distinction from its power of self-moving, is the truth I want to bring out and apply. And how wonderful is this capacity of receiving and appropriating, — simply the faculty of opening the doors and windows of your souls for the Lord to come in, bringing with Him the wealth and glory which He has, that He may make you sharers with Him! Look at this truth in a threefold application.

1. The whole subject of prayer is invested with a living interest, based on the *capacities* of the soul, its receptivity of the Lord. No straining after progress through painful self-culture, no baffled efforts to rise towards God out of yourself. Just keep still, and lay the hush of silence on all your turbulence, and open the door towards Him, and He comes; not by noise, nor by voices, nor by visions, but by a growing peace and confidence and trust, worth more than they, and which, in times of suffering or times of sorrow, come sweetly as an even-song over tranquil waters. You have never found, perhaps, this place of refuge? Well, it is because you never sought it; or, if you did seek it, it was too exclusively through self-culture and self-development. It was because you shut yourself in, and never opened your mouth that He might fill it. The answer to prayer as it comes without, in giving rain, or in healing disease, or in suspending or adapting to us

the laws of the natural world, is a theme on which men raise subtle questions, or on which the scientists apply their prayer-gauge; but all this touches not the heart of the matter. The answer to prayer comes primarily and vitally within; and the only gauge we can apply to it is in the peace that passeth understanding, and the soul laid at rest on the bosom of the Divine Love. It is not a painful flight towards God, but simply a reception of Him. It does not ask of you great things nor difficult things: it asks you to keep still. It is not scaling some transcendent height: it is opening a door. Sometimes prayer is too deep, too earnest, and too still, for words; and sometimes the Lord compels us to be still in order that He may get a hearing in us; lays us on some bed of sickness, that He may stop our noise and get a hearing in us; takes our earthly props away, that we may lean back upon Him; hushes dearly-loved voices in death, that his voice may become more distinctly audible; by all methods of his Providence, seeking to make us know, not merely our power of doing, but our capacity for receiving, and use it till the doors and windows are all open for Him to enter in. And prayer the most effectual is not where there is shouting, and importunity, and endless repetition, as if trying to storm the throne of God, and bring Him down, which some people mistake for earnestness. It is where all our noise and outcries have sunk into calm; and then, when our minds and hearts all open towards Him in our stillest and most listening moods, He comes on like the dawn of the morning, till his light has flushed our whole sky with its colors, and sent into our hearts its exceeding and abiding peace. It is not any self-chafings, nor any storming of the heights: it is simply an opening and a reception; but, in order to this, be sure you put the finger of silence on all your selfish passions and outcries. "Be still," He says, "and know that I am God."

2. Apply the subject, again, to the Divine Revelations. There are two views on this subject,—one based on the intrinsic native ability of human nature, the other based on its faculty of reception. By looking exclusively on man's native abilities, we come to believe that human nature develops upward into Christ's, and produces Bibles from within; and that these are the production of its original and intrinsic powers. Revelation is, according to this view, our own human discovery, as we scale the heights of heaven, and survey the prospect. But the view of man as a recipient shows, that, while man's original power of discovering Divine Truth is very small, his faculty of recognition and reception of truth when given to him is very great.

And here let me give you an historical fact. One fact sometimes is worth more than a dozen theories.

The fact is this. In all the history of the race, no instance has ever been known of a nation really savage rising of itself into the light of civilization, or reaching the higher truths through self-development. Nations sink from civilization into barbarism: they never rise by their native impulsions and abilities out of barbarism into Divine Light. One such case clearly pronounced is yet to be found. On the other hand, carry the Divine Revelation to these people, and see their faculty of reception. The Sandwich Islander, from immemorial time, lived in dread of the demon who inhabited the neighboring volcano. The missionary brought to him a revelation of God, and of his Christ. The demon went out as the Christ came in; and the infernal shadow passed off from the fields, and from the mind of the native, which woke to the consciousness of a new spiritual life. How long, think you, before he would have reached this result by trying to lift himself into the light? The Saxon race, to which we all of us belong, have no difficulty in electing between the worship of Odin and the worship of the God and Father of our Lord Jesus Christ, whose word came to them from Palestine, and found them. But if it had not found them, you and I to-day, instead of being gathered here for worship, might be quaffing from human skulls libations to the war-god of the north, or we might be, by blood and rapine, earning our heaven in the halls of Valhalla. Such is the difference between our original powers of self-development and discovery, and our capacity of reception and appropriation of Divine Truth; between our reason groping its private and solitary way, and our reason penetrated and folded in the Divine Splendors.

The religion of humanity, as the resultant of its own efforts at discovery, has always been either blank atheism or blind superstition. The religion of humanity, as the resultant of Divine Reason and the human, one acting upon the other and within it, is a sublime faith that regenerates and saves. Neither you nor I would ever have discovered the future life; and our private reason groping after it would have flapped its wings among chimeras as dark and vain, probably, as those which the savages chased after. And yet that life may be so unveiled to us that the blazon shall be its own irresistible evidence; for it lifts up the reason when it comes in the transfigurations of its own glory, shows us this life and the other, which before lay dark, dead, and fragmentary, brought into symmetry and order and organic unity, — a unity quite undiscoverable by the faculties of the mind, but recognizable when presented to the open gaze.

While, therefore, our power of original discovery is very small, our faculty of recognizing the truth when it comes, and knowing it when presented, is our most auspicious endowment. It is opening the mouth to be filled with bread from heaven. It is the soul finding its own through the tender Divine adaptations to its profoundest needs. As light to the eye, as music to the ear, as food and drink to him who hungers and thirsts, so, to the reason and to the heart, is truth when unveiled in its benignity and comprehension. What I know of God, and of his will, and of my own destiny, yea, of this very world I live in, by merely diving into myself, or looking through my narrow horizon, would be extremely meagre. What I know, as given to me in the Christ, extends the horizon beyond the grave, and beyond the stars, and lets in the sunlight on my private imaginations, ventilating the little house I live in with the airs of Paradise.

3. Apply this subject in yet another direction. The virtues and the graces of the Christian life, the beautiful flowering and fruitage of Christian believing, are one thing as coming from your receptivity of the Lord, quite another matter as the fruits of mere self-culture and self-development. Humility is one of the prime Christian graces; and it has small chance of cultivation till we acknowledge ourselves recipients of the Lord, till we seek to find Him, by letting Him come to us rather than by building our Babels up towards Him, and trying to scale his heavens thereby. Humility is not humiliation nor

self-disparagement. It is simply rendering to the Lord what belongs to Him, instead of claiming it as our own. We are the most humble when we think least of ourselves, or put ourselves out of the account altogether, and let the Lord shine through us with his uncolored sunlight, without staining it with our own miserable selfhood. As recipients of Him, we own nothing, and therefore have nothing to be proud of. For the gifts and graces of Christian character in which He clothes us, if He clothes us at all, are the radiations of his own life in us; and these are brightest and most heavenly when we are least conscious thereof. As to that life which comes to us by prayer, as to that light of Divine Revelation which folds our reason in a higher wisdom, there is no room for comparison of one man with another, and the strut of our vanities looks hideous indeed.

> "We are all beggars : poor and bare
> We stand before thy face,
> Save when in borrowed robes we flare,
> Or shinings of thy grace."

"Open thy mouth, and I will fill it." The sermon would be but poor preaching if it failed to urge its lesson upon those of you who keep yourselves shut in till you shut God and his revelations clean out. I have thought, sometimes, that Unitarians needed a new Channing, to set forth the receptive capacities of the human soul over against its inherent dignity and power; since its dignity and power only come by its opening to the Lord and his Word, as the buds of spring-time open to the sun and the rain, and thence take on all their greenness and glory. I do think there is less earnest and systematic study of the Bible among us than among any other class of Christian believers. What vast resources has the Christian Sabbath which we have never yet used! One sermon a week, which must be sensational in order to be interesting, — in other words, very discursive and very shallow, — affords small means for any adequate knowledge of the Divine contents of Revelation. The Bible-class, grouping not the children only, but the congregation, with the aids of modern science for the new interpretation, might put us in the way of some more adequate and progressive knowledge of the Divine Word, and would show us I am persuaded, what truths had waited within its covers for our reception. What progress has been made during the last twenty-five years in religious knowledge, especially on the subject of the future life and its relations to this life, clearing away the gloom of death, and the darkness of the grave! It is not that any new revelation has been made, but that the old Bible was full of revelations which people slept over, and would not see. And still it speaks to the condition of our toiling humanity; and while science is doing its best, and remains dumb touching the great problems of eternal life, the invitation is, "Open thy mouth, and I will fill it." And the call to prayer is not a call to exercise some rare gift of volubility, but a call rather to suppress it, and listen at the open door. "Behold, I stand at the door, and knock. If any man hear my voice, and open the door, I will come in, and sup with him, and he shall sup with me."

# SUCCESS.

JOHN XIX. 30: "It is finished."

I DO not understand these words to mean merely, as some expositors would make them, "Life is now at an end: death has come." The Saviour means, "This gives completeness to my work and mission here on the earth." How constantly He sets forth the fact that He was not to die till his hour had come! And even when the dangers and the plottings grew thick around Him, there was always a way of escape through them, until the work He came to do had been accomplished. Not only his death, but the time and method of it, He takes up into his plan, and organizes as one of the factors in working out the grand results of his mission. Once his enemies have Him apparently in their power; but He glides out of their hands, because "his hour had not yet come." And, when the time had arrived, how triumphant is his language! "Father, the hour is come. Glorify thy Son, that thy Son also may glorify Thee." At the beginning, he forecasts his work, and maps out the plan of it. His ministry fills it out, and rounds it into completeness. And so the last words on the cross, "It is finished," announce the consummation on earth of a life which has passed through all its stages, and has been rounded out to its full period. "It is finished." That is not a despondent, but an exultant annunciation; as if He had said, "Now this life, as to its earthly course, sounds the key-note of its consummation and triumph."

We are prone, I think, to let our faith run into belief in special providences, as if God had a special plan for some to work in, and held them to it, while others were outside of it. Rather, we should believe that the great and illustrious ones, and especially the Christ, are the very ones who bring the laws of the Divine Providence into most shining manifestation, — those same laws that infold you and me; and that of every one who lives a Christian life, and does its work, those same words, "It is finished," can be spoken only as sounding the key-note of its consummation and triumph. Hence, you find that those men who have felt themselves called to a special work have had a kind of intuitive consciousness that they were leading a charmed life, that they were believers in predestination; as Murray said when his enemies assailed him, "I am immortal on the earth, so long as God has work for me; and when He has not, I no longer wish to live."

But here a subject of vast and vital interest opens

before us. What is a life that is finished? What do we mean, or what should we mean, by those words, "*success in life*"? No words are more common on the lips of men, in those questionings which arise about the prosperity of each other, than these: "How has the man succeeded?" And prayer for that success is the first which the parent sends up to the throne when his children go forth amid the conflicts and the buffetings of this world. And our feelings of commiseration are never so full as when, musing over the end of life, we cannot say, "It is finished;" but, "It is a failure." He has not overcome the world, but the world has overcome him; and there he lies.

But what is a finished life? Finished in the Christian sense, copied down from that great master-life of all, so that there is neither excrescence nor deficiency; but, like the statue which the sculptor clips and finishes, it is handed over without deformity to its place.

Now, there are two classes of persons, two orders of lives, which have their beginnings in this world. There are those which have no probation here, which are taken out of this world before the period of moral choosing, and whose probation falls on the other side, — infancy and childhood removed to that other sphere, like flowers transplanted to a warmer and more genial clime because the winds in this were too cold and bleak for them.  These are without moral probation here.  But all the others — and, upon the whole, the more favored ones — enter upon a period of moral choice; and of these it must be said by all who believe in a Providence, that, the choice being rightly made, there is no possibility of an untimely end.

This question of a finished life has two answers, — a negative and a positive one.

Its completeness, let us observe in the first place, does not depend upon its duration.  There may be a beautiful completeness in one's life, even when its sun goes down before noon; because it may course its way under suns that come down from a higher sky.  The man, we may suppose, had his object: he lived for it, and he accomplished it; and what more could he have done in this respect, if he had lived a thousand years?  The greatest life ever lived on earth was only thirty years in length.  Others may go on to fourscore and fivescore years, and leave not a trace behind them.  Time with God is nothing, as we measure time; for He measures life only by the events and stages that make up its transitions and periods, not by months and years.

Again: success is not that sort of independence which some people dream of, when they will be free from the anxieties of want, of misfortune, and of temporal change.  Some such goal as this often presents itself to the golden visions of those who are entering on the work of life. That end of pecuniary independence attained, it may be an aid to success, or it may end as most wretched failure; for do you not observe that people who are over anxious to obtain a competence form a habit of anxiety, and are just as anxious about keeping it after they have got it, and just as anxious lest some breath should blow it all away? Nor yet, again, is it worldly position, about which there is so much strut and strife under the disguise of conceit and vanity. Position in the world comes under the arrangements of God, whose laws and conditions we have not the making of; comes when posts of duty are to be filled, and draw to them the men or women who will fill them well. All other positions have only pasteboard and filigree under them; and even the world sees this, and shakes them down with its laughter.

1. But to advance from the negative to the positive side of my subject, we observe, with the great example before us, that every life that ends complete must begin with a Divine mission and purpose. I mean by Divine mission, that its work must be chosen under the recognition of a Providential guidance. Always there is a baptism and a consecration to some work distinctly placed in view and held there. There is a baptism by the Jordan, and a voice from heaven urgent upon the soul, before our probationary life has a beginning, to say nothing of its middle and

its end. I have heard of preachers who had a "call." But there is a special call to every individual, into some work best adapted to the faculties which God has given him, and the opportunities which God has thrown in his way. But, oh, the men and women that float upon the stream of time, and tend no-whither, solely for want of this self-direction and consecration! The reason that is generally given for living without an aim is, that there is no work to do. Every calling is crowded and full; and some persons are crowded out. The plea always and everywhere of our indolence and pride! There is always plenty of work in this world, and more than enough, for all the people who live in it; but some of the work is humble, — brings no honor nor applause, albeit there is no work in all the myriad functions ordained by God which is not sweet and beneficent. But those that aim at nothing, always do nothing, or else they roam from one thing to another; and they never begin life with the sublime baptism, the voice of whose clearly defined purpose so wakes up the faculties, that it rings through the consciousness like the voice that came down on the baptismal waves, "This is my beloved Son."

Here, again, the example of Christ illumines the way of all who follow Him. He is the Messiah, the Sent, the Anointed; so called, because the one great work was given Him to do, and he was born into it and prepared for it; anointed, sent, came even for this cause into the world. It burned in his consciousness clearer and clearer, till it came as a voice from heaven. Down in his own humble sphere, and doing the business of life, — that business being consecrated to a Divine end, — every follower of Christ may see his own work copied down on a lower plane from this Divine example; and then all his work will be holy.

2. After a mission and a purpose, comes a second condition, if life is to be finished or rounded to its close, — a religious faith that will enlighten that purpose and inspire it, and keep it clear and strong. A man must not only aim at something, but he must have such light and guidance that he can hit the mark. He must not work blindly, nor in the dark. No man's life is successful until he has obtained clear and settled religious convictions which illustrate its meaning. He has not succeeded until he has grappled with that problem which meets him at every turn, and which demands a solution of the mystery of existence. I do not mean that a man's creed must all be settled, but he must stand on some fundamental truth which reveals to him the purpose of all our struggles and labors. A man without a religion that solves this problem, is one whose mind is afloat, and who has nothing to guide him through the world's commotions and revolutions. He has no true success

until he is grounded on those everlasting principles which partake not of the vicissitudes of earthly things. Until this be done, he can have no sense of personal security and no unfailing peace. Indeed, a man has never become successful until his essential happiness is placed beyond the reach of all outward fluctuation and change. This can never be done until he has settled with himself what is the true end of life; until, in short, he has embraced a religion on whose solid foundations he feels secure. He may be ever so successful in the competitions of business, and life still remain to him an enigma; and mystery may hang like a dark spirit over all his prospects. What is the end of all this? why are all these struggles and endeavors? are the questions which must haunt him and press upon him in thoughtful hours. Faith, — faith that penetrates the future, and brings down from heaven a bright and blessed philosophy which flings its illuminations over the present scene, and reveals the grand object of all existence, — is essential to true success and victory. It need not be an obtrusive or a difficult faith: its first truths may be as simple as the lessons of a child; but without it there is deceitfulness and hollowness in all prosperity, which then determines to no sublime ends and issues, therefore has no moral unity.

In the whole history of the world, I do not know of any period over which there broods so thick a darkness, as that which just preceded the coming of Christ, when the old religions had failed, and the new religion had not yet dawned. Men of thought groped about, and wondered what they lived for. If for time only, why these yearnings irrepressible, and why these frightful disorders and sufferings? If there is a God, said they, beyond that sky over our heads, why does He not make a rent through it, and tell us for what He made us? Well, God spake through that brazen sky, and the message came; and look a few years later, and you see those communions called Christian churches, dotting the darkness; just as sometimes, when travelling at night, you come in sight of a town that looms up in the distance, and flings its streamlets of light from a thousand windows into the darkness. So Christianity came, revealing a sublime purpose in human existence, and making every man a missionary to his time, for healing its miseries, and rolling the darkness away.

3. I remark, in the third place, and lastly, this life has its completeness when it has prepared us for that higher and better life whose scenes are in prospect. It is complete, that is, when a man has become fit to render it up. This world, in connection with a higher one, is a school of discipline which has certain lessons to be learned, and certain acquisitions to be made, that we may be prepared for the untasked industries of heaven. In this vast and comprehen-

sive economy of Divine Providence, how beautiful and orderly would seem all its operations could we see the whole! — one sphere rising above another, far away towards the central light and glory, each in the lower sphere preparing for the one which is next above him, while the Creator sees all below rising in unbroken gradations toward Himself. Now, there is a time when the soul here on earth is matured for its immortality; and, when that time comes, death is a most auspicious event, for it comes with the angelic annunciation, "It is finished." And yet, when men talk about preparation for death, how liable they are to fall into the cant of sect, or into dark and wildering superstitions! Pious words, mysterious rites, sacred magic of some kind, are substituted for that Christian preparation which gives to life a Divine completeness.

This preparation for a higher life which makes us fit to render up the earthly life, and which makes our probation successful, is exceedingly well defined. It is described as "overcoming the world," "obtaining the victory." In other words, it is when, in that struggle which is going on with every man, between the higher and the lower nature, the former has prevailed, and its principles have been finally established. It is not moral perfection, it is not vicarious righteousness, nor magical faith. It is, in one word, "victory," "overcoming." Plainly, overcoming the world is bringing into subjection those dispositions and passions which the world excites, and to which its corruptions make their appeal. Instead of ruling, they serve. Instead of their overcoming us, we have overcome them, and held them to their place. It is when the awful power of moral choice has been put forth, and you have taken for your rule of life the Divine Law, and not the irresponsible and selfish will. How anxiously must the guardian heavens watch in us that moment of decisive choice, when it comes down clear, decisive, and final, and there is no longer any trembling of the balance! If you have never made this choice, you can make it now, this morning, if you will, with all consecrating vows and prayers. And then there is joy in heaven; and if ever they ring the bells there, it is when a soul is thus gained for its abodes. Because heaven is passing into our minds, not with great noise and commotion, but with broader, clearer, deeper demonstrations of its power and influence, and opposing principles grow feeble, and their murmurs become still. Or else the world is encroaching upon our whole natures, and the higher and heavenly is suffering eclipse and extinguishment under the encroaching shade. It is when the balance has ceased to tremble, and to render the issue doubtful; when God, not self, has become supreme and regnant within,— that man is said to overcome the world. And this is victory; and it was the victory, not over death, but over sin, which called out that burst of gratitude from the apostle, "Thanks be to God that giveth us the victory through our Lord Jesus Christ." And you see this does not depend upon length of years. You who have become old enough to make a clear choice between Christ and the world, that is, to have a probation, can have this victory now, this very day, if you have not already obtained it.

The business of life well chosen, a religious faith that inspires it and keeps it to unselfish ends, the world overcome and under our feet, these three things make up a Christian life that is finished, — finished, I mean, in the sense that life is a heavenly success. And now let me run out and make good another comparison between the life of the Divine Master and the life of all his followers. It is one which the Christian believer cannot meditate without a thrill of triumph and rejoicing. We have seen how, through all the snares of his enemies, Jesus walked secure and serene until he could say, "The hour is come." Till then they had no power over Him. There was no special Providence in his case; for no Providences are special. Only in Him as the Divine Humanity, the great laws of Providence, as they apply to all humanity, blaze forth and become manifest. So it is with every life consecrated to Him, and going on to be finished. It will not, can not stop an hour too soon or an hour too late. Of its day and of its hour no man knoweth. But do not suppose that God knoweth not its hour, nor that that thing of Divine workmanship — a Christian life — better than all the finishings of human art, will fail for want of time. Concealed in the Divine protection, it flows on till its end is gained; for God never leaves his work half done. Choose your work with vows of consecration, do it in the light of a clear faith, and your hour comes not till God, if not man, can write over your grave, "It is finished." Finished, it may be, like the Master's, in the midst of manly vigor and bloom; finished, nevertheless, as that Divine workmanship which God has moulded consummately for the skies. And this it is which gives to the Christian that sense of Divine shelter in storms and in calms which enables him to tread with even pace along all the pathways of this world.

John Wesley, six days before his death, wrote a letter to Wilberforce, the last words of his pen. "I know," he says, in substance, to the philanthropist, "that you must have been raised up for your work and protected in it by God, else you would long ago have been overcome by the men and devils who oppose you." It was the same Providence that guards the lives of its own, until their lives are all complete. I do believe that many a life has come to its end here sooner than it should, because it had no moral purpose; because there was help needed, and work to do, which ought to have drawn out and absorbed the energies which otherwise flowed inward to breed morbid conditions and death to the body and the soul. And so the Lord sponged it out of the world as of no use in the world. And many others have been kept here solely by means of a moral purpose. The vow had been made, "I see a good here I want to work out, and feel called to do;" and the Lord answered, "Take your time for it. Go and do it, and then come up higher."

My hearers, are you living for any thing? Have you begun life with any moral object and end? Have you that faith which will give you guidance, and be a light to go before you as a pillar of flame? Or, are you living without any faith, without any religion, following your calling mechanically, only that you may eat, drink, and sleep? Without some faith to give me a theory of life, as well as its hard and dusty realities, I should feel, as it seems to me, for every grave I saw opened, for every pang that is felt, for every family that passes away, as if I were placed in a world where all is disorder and illusion, —

"To know delight but by her parting smile,
To toil, and wish, and weep, a little while."

Do not deem life successful till the promise is

fairly yours, "He that overcometh, the same shall be clothed in white raiment; and I will not blot out his name out of the book of life, but I will confess his name before my Father, and before his angels."

# THE THREE ADVENTS.

MATTHEW XXV. 13: "Watch! for ye know neither the day nor the hour wherein the Son of man cometh."

THE discourse of our Saviour which comprises the twenty-fourth and twenty-fifth chapters of Matthew's Gospel, is the longest that we have reported, and most remarkable for its solemn grandeur. To fully enter into its meaning, we must stand with the Saviour on the summit of Mount Olivet, just east of the city, overlooking its buildings and its busy population. It is eventide. The most conspicuous object is the temple on Mount Moriah. Its gilded roof and white marble columns would be furbished in the rays of the setting sun. "Ye admire all these things," said Jesus; "but I say unto you, the building shall be razed to its foundations." The disciples are eager to know when this shall be. It shall be at the second coming of the Son of man; and they ask what are to be the signs of that coming. Then begins the discourse which ends with the twenty-fifth chadter. Jesus rises into the highest realm of prophetic vision, and paints with divine pencil the events which foretoken his coming, that coming itself, and its consummation. The commentators, in attempting to analyze this high utterance, find themselves baffled and confused. One view confines the whole prophecy to temporal events,— the destruction of Jerusalem, and the dispersion of the Jews. Another view goes farther. The second coming was the spread of his religion in the world. Another goes farther yet. The second coming is to wind up human affairs. It is a coming to judgment, and to determine the destiny of the race. Take either view, and apply it exclusively, and you will see how it halts and fails. Neither one satisfies all the language and the imagery. Put them all together and they do no more than that. Remember, that from our Saviour's point of view, rapt into the vast future, time ceases to be. Scenes of this world and of the other rise in the perspective, — one in the foreground; the other, dissolving views of the same picture. Scenes of time and eternity shade one into the other; and as all to Him was a present reality, He does not mark the transitions by dates and years.

There is, however, one dominant idea which tones and gives unity to the whole. It is the coming of the Son of man. It is the Divine Advent in Christ. Here, indeed, is the one great truth to which all the leading facts of the Bible history have reference.

Indeed, it is the one truth which unitizes all the history of the world. And what is meant by the coming of the Son of man? Simply God imparting Himself to humanity. Simply the Divine Mind yielding itself to the human mind, in order to cleanse the human, inspire it, and lift it up into the Divine Embrace. But in the accomplishment of this Divine plan there are degrees and stages through which it moves on to its fulfilment.

The coming of Christ is threefold.

His coming in the flesh.

His coming in the soul.

His coming in the judgment, according as He is received or rejected.

His coming in the flesh, we say, for it was necessary that the Divine Word, as the embodiment of the Divine Nature itself, should be made flesh, and appear before the eyes of men, that they might see it living, acting, moving in a human form, and going forth into a perfect human practice. It was necessary, I say, in order to any adequate disclosure of the Divine Nature to men. And why? Because *words alone cannot reveal God.* They may tell us about God, and about his power and majesty, but his intrinsic nature they cannot disclose. We call God our Father, but that word reveals no *Divine* Fatherhood, unless our human relations have been purged of self, and thrill with the Divine Love. Till then those relations are shaped only by the instinct of the natural man. The Jews called Him Father, but that described Him only after their notions of fatherhood; and they were a people who punished their own children with death, and who killed their prisoners of war, even the women and the little ones. What does fatherhood signify among a people whose human relations all have the taint of selfishness? They called Him merciful; but what does mercy mean among people whose mercies are cruel? They called Him good; that meant kind to family and friends, and to nobody beyond. They called Him just; their justice required eye for eye, and tooth for tooth, and personal retaliation, which had in it the deadly taint of hatred and revenge. Words alone cannot reveal God, simply because all human speech has its roots in human experiences and passions, and therefore has the taint of our human imperfection and depravity. The missionary goes among savage nations. He tries to translate the Divine Law into the savage dialects, and finds they have not scope of meaning enough to take it in. The Christian ideas of forgiveness, love, mercy, compassion, have no equivalent where there has been no corresponding experience; and so they float in the air without any roots to be engrafted on, and to give them a resting place. Pile up the words as you may, and string out the adjectives to any length you please, in descriptions of the

Divine attributes, you cannot make them redolent of the Divine charms and glories, because the words can reach no height above the human nature in which they have their root, and out of which they draw up all their meaning and inspiration. Therefore, language alone, gathered from all the dialects of the earth, could not yield to human thought the immaculate conception of the Godhead.

No. Nor could any angel from heaven do it. An angel might have descended, and proclaimed the gospel from the tops of the mountains, and the beautiful vision would have floated in air; but how could it get down to the earth as a fixed and historic reality? What language could the angel have spoken, that the earth would understand? What words in which to translate his ideas, and give them complete body and clothing, could he have found in our dialects down here in the flesh and in the dark? His gospel message would have floated over us as a strain of music, and then died away; hovering above the earth like a song, but having no such articulation and form as to give it an abiding-place among our gross and palpable realities. Words again, angelic words; but words untranslatable into our human speech, because they have no roots in our human experience and history. Indeed, angels did come in this way, all along the ages, and through all the Old Testament history, giving men dreams of a better state, and prophecies of a more glorious future. And the dreams and the prophecies sank down straightway into carnal conceptions of a temporal Messiah. Never were these conceptions dissipated, and our human thought lifted up to the Divine Idea, until, at last, the angel song floated over Bethlehem, and the star stood still over the heavenly babe lying in a manger. And then the Word was indeed made flesh. Not a humanity corrupt and sinful, and which had tainted the very language of human intercourse, but a humanity without any spot on its disk, became the resplendent image of the Divinity. The Divine Word was made flesh. He not only spake, but He assumed human relations, wants, sufferings, temptations, affections, and joys; wrapped the garment of our infancy about Him, as well as that of our childhood and manhood; put on our mortality, and put it off again, in order to show death as the inverse side of resurrection and eternal life. All those goodly words whereby we describe the Divine attributes, — justice, mercy, forgiveness, and love, — He has filled out with new meaning, lifting up our low and sensuous vocabularies into the Divine Light, and breathing the Divine Life into them. They have the taint of our selfishness taken clean out of them; and humanity, in Christ made perfect and Divine, becomes the complete representation and transparency of the Godhead. And so the historic Christ, standing in the midst of the ages, is a twofold revelation. He is the revelation alike of perfect Divinity and perfect humanity; for one is the image of the other, copied down to us out of heaven. He shows us the God we ought to worship, and brings Him nigh, in order that his attributes, though in finite degree, may be formed in us, and we be made partakers of the Divine Nature, and the image of the Divine Perfections.

No religion, before the advent of Christ, ever produced a purer code of morals than did the religion of Buddha. None ever conceived more truly the moral attributes of a perfected human nature. But it had no power, nor has it any to this day, to give those attributes any such incarnation on the earth, or to put human nature in such correspondency with the Divine, as to give the worshipper an adequate conception of the Godhead, or to bring down the Divine energies into man, as the working force of human progress, aggressive and triumphant over evil and sin. The highest state it can produce is a delicious quietism. It is a narcotic to dull the sense of pain, not a cleanser, a stimulant, an inspirer, and a call to victory; because, in the place where God should be, it left a blank spot in the heavens. It was a waiting, a listening, a prophecy, towards the fulness of time, when, through this painful void, the tidings should come down, and the Christ should appear as the manifestation of the Divine Personality.

But the historic Christ is not enough. Models of perfection, human or divine, are not enough. The Christ of eighteen hundred years ago must be also the Christ of to-day, if He would be to us a living Saviour and Redeemer. Patterns of perfection away back in the centuries, however lofty and resplendent, what are they to me so long as I cannot lift myself up to them out of my own weakness and sin? The historic Christ were not enough; therefore Jesus speaks constantly of a second coming, more inward and spiritual. "I go away, that I may come again." "I will come again unto you." "The Holy Spirit was not yet, because the Son of man was not glorified." "If I go not away, the Comforter will not come; but if I depart, I will send him." In other words, "I go away to be nearer to my disciples on the spiritual side, and to be to them a Mediator, through whom the Holy Spirit yields itself to human nature, to cleanse it, and renew it, and shape it in the Divine Image." Christ merely as an example would only hold out to us patterns of perfection to dazzle and mock us. To follow Him only as a model man, would make us the mere mimics of his virtues; yea, it were a fantastic endeavor to put on a righteousness that never would fit to us, and which we never could wear; for who is the man that can do the things that He did, and who can use his speech? *Inspiration*, not imitation, is our prime need, as the disciples of the Lord Jesus Christ, and the need of his church as an organism fitted to receive Him, and to embody his power and spirit on the earth. Our prime need is a new influx of power, not from Christ crucified, but from the Christ risen and glorified, and inspiring his church to-day. His first coming was to put men in right relations to each other, to install a society and brotherhood purged of the old corrupt selfishness, consecrated to God and humanity; in fine, a church into which He could come, and which He could fill with Himself. That done, the Holy Spirit could descend, and sweep the human heart like a lyre. For man must be in right relations with his brother, before he can be in such relations with God as to commune with Him, and receive his spirit. There must be a true brotherhood and fellowship, or there can be to us no Divine Fatherhood and communion, out of which the Holy Spirit can descend to mould us anew in the Divine Image. And just in the degree that the Christian church has been such a brotherhood and fellowship, has the promise of Jesus been fulfilled, "Lo, I am with you alway;" and the Christian communion and confession have been impleted with the power, the comfort, and the fire, of the Holy Ghost. The discipleship which is a whole consecration to Christ as a Mediator and Saviour, present in his church to-day, melting through all its rituals, and melting the ice out of its fellowship, is never without the Comforter. And then He clothes us, not with any imputed righteousness put on from without, but with a real, intrinsic righteousness inspired from within; and then obedience is a delight, and duty is a song of praise.

I trust I am speaking to the experience of some of you with whom the Christ of history is the Christ of consciousness; that the power of his resurrection is the power of a Saviour close at hand, melting the heart into contrition and tenderness, hanging the bow of peace on every cloud of sorrow, making your communion-table seem like the gate of heaven, because Christ and the Comforter are there. I believe I am reciting the experience of eighteen centuries, when I say that forms of religion with the Christ taken out of them have the Comforter taken out of them also; and then the words which describe the Divine attributes of Fatherhood become emptied of their meaning, and shade off into the unknowable forces of the universe, and float over us in the wintry air; and then prayer becomes a form, for it takes hold of nothing; whereas, with the Christ of to-day as a Real Presence, the Father is brought wondrous nigh in personal communion, the Divine Heart melts into our hearts till the Divine Love overflows; and the angel song of peace and good-will is the prolonged strain of the centuries, singing itself not in the upper sky, but in the music of the soul, and making communion with God in Christ a prayer without ceasing.

Such are his coming in the flesh, and his coming in the soul, or the Christ of history, and the Christ of consciousness.

But there is described a last stage of the advent of God in Christ, the consummation of the two others. Jesus in this high utterance sees the current of our human life sweeping on beyond the brink of mortality, into the gathering-place of all nations and peoples, — the spirit-world, where the generations pass in continuous processions to the endless abodes. And there He describes yet another coming of the Son of man. It is the Divine Word that comes to judgment, the Eternal Truth that discerns the souls of men, and resolves them into their class and order and place; not by some technical standard, but according as they have been true to the claims of brotherhood and humanity. "As ye have done it unto one of the least of these, ye have done it unto me." "I go to prepare a place for you," and, "I will come again, and receive you unto myself; that where I am, there ye may be also."

The only home of the Christian disciple is where the love of Christ reigns in its fulness. Hence, when this cumbering load of mortality falls away from the disciple, the immortal life will be to him a still nearer and more complete advent of his Lord. The same voice which called him here to self-consecration, is then, "Come, ye blessed, inherit the kingdom." It is not the Christ sitting on an outward throne, and judging by arbitrary law, but the same Word that was made flesh, and which had been the law of the Christian life, and the Christ of experience, now calling by inward attractions to that immortal fellowship whose peoples no man can number. And this is the judgment-seat of Christ, that discerns the Christ-like, and raises them up at the last day. And these are the three advents through which God yields Himself to our humanity, and purges it, and fills it with Himself.

And as the "Come, ye blessed," simply formulates the law of inward attraction that draws heart to heart, and mind to mind, when all the hinderances of earth have fallen away, so the "Go, ye cursed," formulates the law of repulsion with those in whom there is no love of Christ, nor love of his work, but, in place thereof, the selfishness by which men are shut fast in their own prison-house, and preyed upon by its tormenting fires. There is no arbitrary law here. Christ received is heaven commencing now, and consummating in that state where his love reigns supreme. Christ rejected is the rejection of the means of renewal and peace, of all that makes the heavenly communion and the heavenly employments sweet and attractive. The third advent of the Eternal Word reveals every man as he is; and, under its resolving power, every man determines to his own place.

Such, then, is the Divine coming in Christ. How gradually has He melted through the ages, and into the heart of the world! How slowly has his own church understood Him, and received his mind into hers! And yet "the sign of the Son of man in heaven" was never more plain than at the present hour. Never were more auspicious the omens of a new gathering of sects and denominations around his Divine Personality; and here is the central force which is to re-organize and guide the distracted and groping nations. In both hemispheres, the East and the West, the old oppressions are dying, the crushing burdens are being lifted off, the shackles of the slave are melting, the priestly thrones are shaking, the hymns of freedom are ascending, and Christ, in his humble poor, and in his despised ones, is claiming redemption. The real progress of Christianity is to be measured, not so much by its spread outward, as by its descent downward; not through miles of space, but downward from great things to less things, from the heights of the world to its plains and valleys, from Sundays to week days, from the lord to the serf; yea, from man down to the ranks below him, till beast and bird shall rejoice in its protection. From every burden made light, from every soul redeemed from sin and suffering, from any suffering creature whose pangs you have softened or assuaged, comes the Saviour's benediction, "Ye have done it unto me."

Out of every human form, and out of every sentient being, from whose suffering we turn away when the opportunity is offered, comes the same voice, "Ye did it not to me." As the Kingdom of Christ comes in this world, He calls us to work in it and for it; and our acceptance or rejection at last are conditioned, not so much on what we believe about Him, as on our working with Him in full consecration of ourselves. For the "Come, ye blessed," and "Go, ye cursed," enounce the conditions of heaven or hell. What is heaven but a grandly organized beneficence and charity, from which angels come and go on errands of love and redemption? And what is hell but that state where souls are dungeoned up in themselves, because they never saw God in his little ones?

So, let us gather home, to-day, and apply to ourselves, the lesson of this practical Christianity of the sermon on Mount Olivet. "Consecrated" is the word which the Master writes on every faculty of mind and body. Consecrated to Divine ends, to unselfish living, to the filling-up of golden opportunities for lifting the heavy burdens, and for diffusing the love of Christ through the ties of brotherhood that are woven all about us, and for making his image shine brighter in some soul where it was marred and broken. For such is the condition of the benediction, " Come ye blessed ; as ye have done it unto one of the least of these, ye have done it unto me."

# PROGRESS.

PHILIPPIANS III. 12: "Not as though I had already attained, either were already perfect; but I follow after, if that I may apprehend that for which also I am apprehended of Christ Jesus."

PERHAPS a clearer rendering would be: "Not that I have already won, or am already perfect; but I press on, if indeed I might lay hold on that for which Christ laid hold on me."

I understand Paul in this passage to announce the fundamental principle of what we call Liberal Christianity. It is a religion of *progress*, and allows no living believer to be satisfied with present attainments. It supposes that Christianity has dawned upon us as a system so vast and comprehending, that we refuse to fix it in stationary creeds. When we have gained one height which we thought was to be the summit, it only shows us other and sublimer heights beyond, which before had not come into our field of view. For to explain the mysteries of religion does not diminish their number. To throw light on one subject is to bring into contemplation others, which never before had been the object of thought;

even as when the day is chasing back the twilight, the twilight is making the same encroachment on the realm of total darkness.

There are, however, two theories about progress. One leaves Christ behind, and finally gets Him clear out of the way. The other keeps Him on before, a pillar of flame that burns brighter and brighter. Let me characterize both these methods, and so come to the heart of our subject, — Christianity as a liberal or ever progressive faith.

A man opens the New Testament, and finds there a remarkable series of events and characters, called miracles. He never has seen any thing like them, and he cannot believe any thing which has not been compassed by his own experience. His first object, then, will be to bring Christ within our human dimensions, and to disengage and separate the supernatural from the natural; casting out the former, and retaining the latter. But what are the supposed facts thus to be disengaged and thrown away? They pertain to the conception, the birth, the ministry, the works, the death, the resurrection, the ascension, of Jesus Christ, and his second coming in the Paraclete, or Holy Spirit. After these are taken out, what have we left? The discourses. Well, what are the discourses? Nearly all of them grow out of these events, are presupposed by them, and are *founded* upon them. For example: all our Saviour's predictions of his death, resurrection, and second coming at the fall of Jerusalem; and all that discourse about the Comforter He was to send, running through the Gospels and interlacing them; and even the Sermon on the Mount was preached to the multitude which thronged Him on account of his miraculous works. What is there left? Nothing. The Christ has vanished from the theatre of common history into the clouds, and beyond them, and is out of the way altogether. Some are frank enough to acknowledge this as the final result, and accept it. This new theism says, in its last authoritative utterance, "It is time to let Jesus rest. His fame has become a grievance the free spirit avoids. It closes in the heavens, and cuts off communication. It no longer mediates, but separates. Jesus is made a stumbling-block to the generation. As such he impedes progress, and must be removed. Let the people to-day speak of themselves in their own name, in their own spirit." Well, Christ being put out of the way, what do these people tell us about God, about the soul, about immortality? They go on, and use the phraseology of religion, the Holy Spirit, immortality, eternal life. By and by you find that the former meaning of these words has all leaked out of them; and they hang empty, and float in air. The Holy Spirit means, not an influence and energy which comes from above man, and from a personal Deity, but the moral and religious sentiment, self-excited and warmed up within. Immortality means, not a personal existence beyond the grave, but living in the affections and memories of those who survive us. "Many winter storms," says one of these apostles of the new religion, "have swept over the grave of Hegel and Goethe; but does not their spirit still live among us? It is as Christ said, 'Where two or three are met together, there am I in the midst of them.' Thus, each continues to live according to his works." Personally we die, and our consciousness goes out; our qualities survive, to be reproduced in the everlasting tides of the infinite; and this is immortality sublimed by philosophy. This result is not reached all at once; but, outside of the aid of Christian ideas and personalities, men gravitate towards these results as surely as water to its level. Try the experiment. Blot out the Christ, and reconstruct a supernaturalism out of your own mind. Probably it will compare with the immortal realities as the web which the spider weaves out of her own bowels, till she clouds herself all over with it, compares with the great world outside of earth and sky, surrounded by which her little gossamer swings for an hour. It is a very significant fact, that in Germany, long after the idea of a personal Christ, a personal Deity, and a personal immortality had been abandoned by men who professed and even preached Christianity from orthodox pulpits, the old phraseologies and rituals and names kept on just the same. It was some time before it was discovered, on nearer approach and examination, that the citadel was deserted, that the ordnance was all wooden, though painted in exact imitation of the old guns that had been taken down; and that, when you entered through the gates, you found the city evacuated, all its armies and peoples gone, all its stores of provision removed, its streets as silent as a graveyard, your voice echoing back from deserted habitations, and your footfall ringing hollow among the tombs. Such is the Christianity without any Christ in it, and such the kind of progress which it gives us.

A writer gives us a good illustration of this kind of progress. The captain of a coasting-vessel had become weary, and, putting the helm into the hand of a negro servant, retired to his hammock. But, before he retired, he pointed to the North Star, and charged the new helmsman always to keep that in his eye, and steer towards it, and all would be well. But, in the course of the night, the storm came, and the winds blew, and the new helmsman found himself in a general confusion of sails flapping, and ship whirling and reeling and plunging at random. However, he came safe out of the storm, as he thought; and, looking up for his guiding star, found it away behind him, and he was sailing swiftly away from it. Congratulating himself for his rapid sailing, he went below, and woke his master. "I have sailed past the North Star. Please give me another star to steer by." The captain came upon deck, and looked round. "Sailed by the North Star! Don't you see that you have turned right about, and are sailing back where you started from, and are bound for nowhere?" *This* is the progress of men who have sailed by the Star of our immortal hopes and faith and progress, to those realms of emptiness where they ray out their own darkness, and hear no voices but the hollow echoes of themselves.

> "No sail ahead,
> No look-out's saving song:
> Death and the dark across their bows,
> And all their reckoning gone."

Look now one moment at the other kind of progress, — progress within Christianity, and with Christ as the Divine centre of human faith and hope and love.

A Divine work differs from a human in nothing more than in this: that, while our human contrivances appear fair on the surface, they are all surface, and we soon leave them out, and have done with them; whereas a Divine work opens and opens forever, through endless perspectives of beauty. Kepler, who discovered so much that he was far beyond his age, which could not understand him, exclaims in a sort of Divine rapture, "I can wait a hundred years for a reader, since God waited six thousand years for an observer of his works."

It is just so in that other revelation, God revealing Himself in Jesus Christ. If his work had been only a human contrivance, like that of all teachers, can we imagine that eighteen hundred years would have passed away, and, at the end of that time, the choicest wisdom of the world would find that it had learned only the surface of Him, that it had got only a little way beneath the letter of his Word, that still He is so far before the age, and before all ages, that we may say of Him a thousand times more truly than Coleridge said of Milton, that *He dwarfs Himself in the distance?* It is under this conception of Christ and his religion, that Liberal Christianity condemns all attempts to reduce them into a human creed, and so turn them into fossils. "Away with your human creeds!" said Channing: "they come between me and my Saviour, in whom the fulness of the Divinity dwells."

Let us now see what is progress within Christianity, and under the quickening power of its Divine revelations. This progress may be briefly specified under three heads: —

1. Our knowledge of a future life.
2. Our knowledge of God.
3. Our knowledge of ourselves.

1. The progressive knowledge of the world concerning the great themes of immortality, under the steady light of the Christian revelation, shows how inexhaustible are its riches. The age of Christ, and the ages that followed, could not understand Him; and why should they? They were swamped in the senses, and had just begun to feel the motions of a spiritual nature. And so when He promised to come again, and raise the dead, and abolish death, and open the heavens, and receive his saints into glory, they thought He was to raise the dead bodies out of the graveyards at the end of time, and take them up into the sky. How poor and inadequate and sensuous the conception! on a plane of meaning how vastly below that of Christ! And yet, low as it was, what precious immortal truth was housed and protected by it, far above the surrounding paganism in which men were dying without hope, while the great company of Christian martyrs and believers were meeting death with triumphal songs! And so up to this hour all science, philosophy, and discovery have only helped to interpret Christ, and raise the world up to the level of his meaning, and make us wonder we had not seen it before. How progressive has been our knowledge of a future life! And now the shores of immortality, instead of being away over the river, come down to meet us, are firm already under our feet, with no river of death between. Only the frail textures of this

mortal body between, like a tent pitched for a day and a night, whose curtains are only to be folded up to disclose the endless perspectives of immortality. The progress of the Christian faith on this subject has been so gradual and yet so sure, that we hardly perceive the progress; and we have to go back and dig up old sermons, or decipher old tombstones, before we discover how much crude and earthly stuff has melted out of the creeds, and melted away from the imperishable gold. Any little child in the Sunday school knows more to-day on this subject than the collective wisdom of the world in the year one. And when once the connection between this life and the future life is clearly seen and acknowledged as not factitious and arbitrary, but as *organic and vital*, there is hardly an article of the Christian faith which is not shown in clearer illumination. The resurrection, retribution, atonement, heaven and hell, and eternal life, are freed from old errors and absurdities, and begin to disclose their wealth of meaning as never before. Because, if the resurrection means not that of dead bodies from graveyards to a local heaven or hell, but of the immortal man out of his mortal covering to the heaven or hell he belongs to already, and which first enter him before he enters them, there is no longer any place for vicarious atonement, or imputed righteousness, or arbitrary punishments or rewards. Christianity, free of artificial theologies, becomes the universal religion, through which the Christ has ever a new advent to the mind and heart of man. "Lo, I am with you alway!" And still how imperfectly do we compass all the wealth of truth in the words of Jesus, and all that He meant by heaven and hell, and eternal life, and the power of his resurrection! and how fitting still is Paul's language on our lips! — "Not that I have already won, nor am already perfect; but I press on, if indeed I might lay hold on that for which Christ laid hold on me."

2. Again: our *knowledge of God* is steadily progressive under the Christian relation. God is infinite; and the highest angels do not learn Him out. But we get ideas and representations of Him, which draw us ever up into his light and love.

Nature represents Him, but how partially and poorly! Nature, says Agassiz, is the thought of God. That were well enough if Nature gave only images of beneficence and purity. But, if her snakes and reptiles and wolves and destructive poisons are the thought of God, then I despair of any worship through Nature, that opens a way to the infinite Love.

So, too, if our sinful and erring humanity gives us the only opening up into the nature of God, our case is about as bad; for the serpents and the wolves are in that also. But how is it under the Christian revelation? There were three great Sanctities taught by

Jesus, — the Father, the Son, and the Holy Ghost ; and in the name of these He charged his followers to go and baptize the nations. It was inevitable that the world, just emerging from its besotted idolatries, should take these three great Sanctities for three Gods, rather than for the methods of the Divine manifestations. So they did, and so they do still. But, even so, what precious truth was housed and sheltered by them until the time when Christianity by its inherent life should break in pieces the rude coverings which confined it, and the narrow formulas which crippled it! Trinitarianism preserved the great truth of the Divine Personality, without which all worship is only a cry of the bereaved heart into vacancy. Trinitarianism, however lame and imperfect its interpretation, saved the world from an idolatry which was worse than that, and from an atheism which was worse yet, until these three great Sanctities were seen in a higher unity with their fullest revelation and expression in Jesus Christ, the highest form in which God can possibly be symbolized, a perfect humanity as the unclouded image of his attributes. The progressive knowledge of the world and of the Christian Church, towards the highest and purest theism, is here most beautifully illustrated. Not through nature, not through your humanity or mine, tainted with moral corruption, can this highest knowledge be obtained. It is found in the grand composite doctrine of the New Testament, — one God and one Mediator. The first, one God, preserves the Divine Unity; and the intellect is satisfied  The second, one Mediator, preserves the Divine Humanity and Personality; and the heart is satisfied too. I know henceforth that those golden words, justice, mercy, goodness, forgiveness, and love, do not mean one thing as applied to God, and quite another thing as applied to men. I know that the Divine qualities revealed in and through Jesus Christ are all human and personal qualities; and the hard dogmas of Calvinism, and the gilded fog of Pantheism, melt and vanish alike before the warm splendors of that revelation.

3. Lastly, *our knowledge of ourselves.* How little do we know what we are and what we need, until we are brought under the analyzing and searching beams of the gospel of Christ! When we build our theologies out of our instincts alone, they are sure to pamper our pride and self-love. They put man at the centre, and God away off on the circumference. Now Christ must be put out of the way, say some, because the spirit of the age requires it. They assume that they are the age, as the French king assumed that he was the state. This sort of conceit is natural to us; and it is the very stuff which the gospel of Christ first discovers, and sifts clean out of us, giving us the humility of discipleship instead. The highest evi-

dence of Christianity consists in its own power of *finding* men, of cleaving through the incrustations of self and sin, of smiting the rocky heart, and making all the fountains of its love to gush forth. These are the highest miracles of Christianity. Within it and beneath it I become conscious of depravity and want and privation, and a proud, corrupt selfhood. But, under its regenerating and creative power, I see a creation rise out of this chaos, more goodly and fair than the order of external nature; experiences more rich than the regalements of sense; a sunshine from the Divine face, more bright than summer glories; a peace more sweet than the tranquillity of the morning; affections purged of self, and enlarged to universal love; calls to duty more loud and clear than matin-bells, putting all private wishes and passions in the hush of silence; strength to suffer and to do, that comes by prayer; a power back of personal volitions, transfusing the whole being, and creating it anew; convictions of truth growing bright to the perfect day; in storms, a sense of refuge under the shadow of Divine wings. Here are the miracles of Christ; and still He goes before us, and tells us of greater heights to be won. And so we end as we began, with the same words on our lips: "Not that I have already won, or am already perfect; but I press on, if indeed I might lay hold on that for which Christ laid hold on me."

# THE THRONES IN HEAVEN.

REVELATION XX. 4: "I saw thrones."

THRONES in heaven appear often in the imagery of the Seer of the Apocalypse. They appear in gradation, rank above rank; and three grades are defined and distinguished. There is the throne of the Supreme, who sits thereon, encircled with rainbows; and the worshippers rest not, day nor night, saying, "Holy, holy, holy, Lord God Almighty, which was and is, and is to come!"

There is the throne of the Lamb, who receives homage almost as great, who draws around Him the hallelujahs of every creature which is in heaven and on the earth, and in the under-world and in the sea; whose name is coupled with that of God in receiving adoration; who sitteth down on the throne of God, or who is in the midst of the throne, so that the same throne is called *the throne of God and the Lamb*. The same divine predicates are applied to Him as to the Almighty,—Alpha and Omega, the Beginning and the End, the First and the Last. And He feeds the saints from the midst of the throne, and judges the sinners who hide under rocks from the wrath of the Lamb.

Then there is the third and lower rank of thrones, — those of the twenty-four Elders; thrones of judgment for the redeemed who are to reign with Christ; and the promise is given, that, as Christ sits down with the Father on God's throne, so the saints shall sit down with Christ on his throne.

You know very well what some of the literalists make of all this. And, in my judgment. some of the Unitarian literalists make the worst work of anybody. It is the worship of a created being. made *almost* as high as God, but not quite; so exalted that he sits on the throne of the Almighty, and receives worship such as no enlightened pagan ever gave to inferior divinities. Yet it is not supreme worship, they say, but analogous to that paid to sovereigns and magistrates, only more magnificent. as to one whom God has exalted very highly; for, does He not promise the same to his saints who are to sit with Him on thrones of judgment? And what is the judgment seat of Christ, to which his saints, and we his humble followers, are thus supposed to be invited? Turn to the twenty-fifth chapter, and you will see. The Son of man comes in glory to summon all peoples to his bar, sits on the throne of his glory, and separates the saints from the sinners, — those to eternal life, these to eternal punishment: a *very* singular judicial process, if the saints themselves are on the throne of judgment, and not at the judgment bar!

This imagery of the Apocalypse only puts into concrete and objective form the figurative language of Jesus in the Gospels. When events were moving on to their crisis, Peter came to Jesus with the question, " Behold, we have forsaken all, and followed thee: what shall we have therefore?" Then Jesus assures his apostles in reply, " When the Son of man shall sit on the throne of his glory, ye also shall sit upon twelve thrones, judging the twelve tribes of Israel." The ambition of two of them took fire at the prospect. They wanted the highest thrones, one at the right and one at the left of Christ; and, soon after that, the two sons of Zebedee came with their mother secretly, and applied for such promotion. What was the answer of Jesus? One of the most solemn rebukes of human ambition it ever received, and one of the most touching lessons of humility and self-sacrifice : " Whosoever will be chief among you, let him be your servant; even as the Son of man came not to be ministered unto, but to minister. To sit on my right hand and on my left, is not mine to give. Ye shall indeed drink of my cup; but it will be a cup of trembling." Has Jesus left these lessons behind, and gone into the heavens, thence to address a more potent stimulus to our mean selfishness and our pompous vanities than the empty grandeurs of earth could ever give? When we undertake to interpret a symbolical book, we should not mix up symbol and letter into a jumble. What a slough of insane nonsense the Apocalypse has been made of in that way, any one may see by reading over the piles of commentary under which it has been buried. But keep consistently to the symbolic meaning; and then, though we may not be drawn up to its sublime heights of vision, we shall have serene and blissful openings through which come beholdings of truth, as through gates ajar.

Persons in the Apocalypse, and the imagery among which persons appear, symbolize truths, — even Christianity as a system of truth in its power of judging, regenerating, and saving mankind. What are the apostolic thrones? Seats raised aloft, with the fishermen of Galilee robed royally, and sitting thereon as the judges of their fellow-men, — they to whom the first injunction came, "Judge not, that ye be not judged"? Not at all; but the apostolic truths which they represented, applied in their royal power to subdue and to save, and beneath which those twelve men have learned by this time to bring themselves in lowly self-surrender. And what is the worship of the Lamb? Of some created, dependent being, receiving joint honors with God, and while sitting on his throne with the hallelujahs of the universe rising around him? Not at all. It is the worship of God as seen in the Word, the Divine Truth that reveals Him, that Divine Truth which was made flesh, — the worship of God as humanized to our finite conceptions and deepest spiritual needs. Does any enlightened person need to have it proved to him that the " Lamb as it had been slain, seen in the midst of the throne of God," is not letter, but symbol ? — not a Lamb literally, nor a man who had been put to death, but the Divine Nature symbolized to us as Sacrifice, Mercy, and Love, — love so tender that, like our human love, it can be wounded, even bleed for us, can give itself away for our redemption, yea, can be crucified and killed, — killed out from the impenitent soul ; a love of which the sacrifice on Calvary is only an outward sign, but the truest and the tenderest which our earthly annals can afford. Such are the sublime doctrines set forth by these thrones in heaven, — whether they be apostolic, or the throne of God and the Lamb.

But let us come to the great practical lessons which are evolved, and which speak to our condition, from these passages of the Divine Word. There is a lesson of Christian humility, and there is a lesson pertaining to the Christian experience.

1. I saw thrones, — thrones of men who try to sit on the judgment-seat of Christ, or who steal his truth, and try to make it their own, and trick them-

selves out in its splendor and royalty. To preach Christ is to put one's self altogether out of the way, — to hide one's self, as it were, in Him, — so that his word and doctrine may have a more unobscured and perfect forthgoing. When you see a sect or denomination bringing out its great men, who cover each other continually with garments of praise and adulation, you may be pretty sure they are fast losing sight of the Master. How often do these idols appear upon the stage to receive the incense of the hour, and then to be dashed down again, or to be covered with mire when they cease to echo back the adulations, or phrase the notions, of the hour! No surer test could be applied, to determine the state of the times, than, how far *persons* are made to figure in the foreground, and not these great and shining truths before whose coming persons fade out of sight, yea, before which every man becomes great only as he hides himself in those beams in whose shinings he is less than a mote in the waves of a summer's noon. How instinctively do we give the name of "personalities" to those controversies in which men put forward their little selves till they cease to represent ideas! When churches are gathered around men, dependent upon the sensation men can produce, to be played upon by words, or amused by the sky-rockets of eloquence, they are churches no more, but a mob of people to dispute when the show is over, and the rockets have gone out. Oh! I have been to churches where the preaching intellectually was about as poor as it could be, but where the Christ, in his Word, seemed all the more to come in, and thrill every soul as with the pulsings of the Holy Ghost, and where every one had a sense of mingled reverence and delight, as he felt his feet taking hold of the Rock of Ages. What are preachers with their rhetoric, where the heavens are open, and God is coming down, and the great doctrines of Christianity, loud as the sound of many waters, are speaking to the conscience and to the heart, and to the ear of Christian faith, and bringing salvation nigh? I have been to church, too, where there was neither God nor Christ, but where some preacher had usurped the place of both, playing upon crowds without ideas, or with only negative ones, and where the crowd was to melt away to-morrow, like a mob seeking some new diversion.

Only when the apostolic thrones arise in their real grandeur, not thrones of men but thrones of judgment, where Divine Truth sits in its royalty and sovereignty, bringing home to the conscience the meanness of self and the littleness of its pride, and laying it prone in the dust with "God be merciful to me a sinner;" opening the future down the long avenues of its retributions; showing where the ways part up and down, and showing the way to pardon, purity, and peace, — only there are such thrones as are set in heaven. And before these thrones persons disappear and hide themselves; and the voice comes now as ever, "He that is greatest among you, let him be your servant; even as the Son of man came not to be ministered unto, but to minister, and to give his life a ransom for many. Ye shall indeed drink of my cup; but it must be a cup of sacrifice, and, to your ambition and your pride, a cup of trembling."

2. I saw thrones. What thrones does the vision disclose in the opening future? See how the apostolic thrones of judgment have been rising ever since, towering above the strifes and ambitions of men. When St. John had this vision of the future, Rome was ruling the whole world, and the Christian martyrs were pouring out their lives at the foot of the Roman power, and John was in banishment at Patmos. But look down a few years, and behold the change!

> "The Roman Cæsars rule the world,
>   Jehovah's sway is given to Jove:
> But, lo! Christ's standard is unfurled:
>   The eagle cowers before the dove;
> Before the nations' wondering eyes
> The apostolic thrones arise."

And they have been rising ever since higher and higher above the strifes and tumults of this world. The Christian truth, on its throne of authority, has been gaining year by year in its power over persons and personal strifes. The Divine Creed of the Bible, above all private creeds and personal interpretations of it, gains in authority, I think, day by day. It becomes daily more profane to dispute over truths which ought to command us and hold us in reverent awe; before which inquiry and comparison, and mutual help, are the proper attitude, but beneath which personal disputing ought to be hushed as a clap of thunder hushes the noise of a rookery. Why, they talk about the nature of Christ, and the psychology of God, which they propose to analyze as a naturalist would analyze a sea-shell or an insect's wing! To understand Christ, we must follow Him; to know God, we must obey Him, — obey Him in thought and in heart, as well as deed. And then He draws us up into his refuge, and tells us the secret of his nature; for He gives us a living experience of his love.

. 3. I saw thrones. And high above them all is "the throne of God and the Lamb." This it is which is circled with rainbows, token that the storms are over. What an image to symbolize to us, and open out to us, the wealth of the Divine Nature in all its goodness and tenderness! No wonder that St. John dwelt upon the image so fondly. He had walked with Jesus through the fields of Esdraelon, where the shepherds lead the flocks beside the still waters. There he had seen the shepherds carry the lambs in their arms, and feed them. He had seen the lamb offered in sacrifice on the altar. All this imagery passes into his vision; and he looks up, and sees the Lord of heaven no longer as on Sinai, clothed in lightnings, but clothed in rainbows, and imaged forth as Sacrifice, Mercy, and Peace. Type and symbol, too, of the Christian experience; for when our angers, our strifes, our passions, keep us away from Him, He is a consuming fire. His nature and ours are in lurid antagonism. We may talk of the love of God, but it turns to lightning around us. Come to Him in filial obedience and self-surrender, and before long you look up, and there are thrones in heaven, and above them all is the throne of God and the Lamb, and all around it are the rainbows of Peace. Then and there we enter the still region that lies away from broils, and, in the full experience of the Divine forgiveness, we sing our Coronation Song : —

"Worthy is the Lamb that was slain, to receive power and riches, and wisdom and strength, and honor and glory, and blessing; for Thou hast redeemed us to God by thy blood, out of every kindred and tongue and people and nation."

# PEACE BY POWER.

MATTHEW X. 34: "I came not to send peace, but a sword."

EIGHTEEN hundred years of conflict is the summing-up of the external history of Christianity. There have been intervals of peace; but these intervals have been of the nature of a truce rather than of a settled and universal amity. Some of the great wars, modern and mediæval, may be traced directly or indirectly to the new element which Christianity has brought in for working out the civilization of modern times. Our war of independence could never have taken the form it did, perhaps would never have occurred at all, had some of the first principles of the gospel not been involved in it; and our late civil war was an open and direct conflict of Christian civilization with the old barbarism which sought to quench the light of that civilization in Christian blood.

For, what is the element which Christianity has brought into the world, and which struggles for supremacy? It is the worth of man. It is the new and higher valuation placed on the human soul. It is the worth of man, not merely as a part of the state, nor as a subject of government and a means to its temporal ends; but his worth individually and personally, having in himself an end, to accomplish which, both Church and State are, or should be, means and helps. The Christ reveals to the individual consciousness a capacity and destiny reaching beyond time into the endless future; and reveals that the highest offence against God and humanity is to violate the conditions of human development and progress. To restore the Divine image in the soul, and show the worth of human nature for endless progress and enjoyment, and remove out of the way every thing that hinders their realization, — it was for this that Christ came into the world. But what loads of effete superstitions were piled upon the soul, and were crushing it into the dust! what hoary despotisms, both Jewish and pagan! What revolutions must be set going, heaving society from its old foundations, what commotions, what wars in divers places, before the burdens could be lifted off, and the soul be set free on its upward way! The vast multitude of human beings were but as the swarms of a day, before the tyrannies of the age; but, in each individual of those multitudes, Christianity revealed a royalty which in the eye of God outshone all the grandeurs of earth.

Of course, the first thing Jesus brought was a sword. Not in his own person, not girded with it

Himself, nor binding it on his disciples. This plainly is not his meaning. On the contrary, his charge to his disciples was, "Be ye wise as serpents, and harmless as doves." But He caused it to be brought. He furnished the occasion of its flashing from innumerable scabbards, with the purpose of cleaving down this new religion which put the human soul above all temporal interests and royalties, and bade them serve and do it homage. It was drawn first on Himself. The Jewish ecclesiasticism was already undermined by Him. He had inaugurated a moral revolution that was rolling from Galilee up to the capital, and rolling under it. The priesthood must go down, or Christianity must. It was Calvary over against Mount Moriah. It was the invisible New Jerusalem against the old Jerusalem. And it has been Calvary ever since, — Calvaries all over the earth, where the New Jerusalem has been descending and bringing redemption to the soul, — over against the old Jerusalem which wields the sword against it, but in vain.

Such, it seems to me beyond question, is our Saviour's meaning in the text where He is putting his religion over against the false religions which were to oppose it, and try to extinguish it in its own blood. It would divide friends, neighbors, families; for the new converts would come out of all conditions. The new gospel would take a deeper hold of human nature than any natural or earthly ties, parting men by new divisions right and left, leaving the old heathenism and Judaism on one side, and on the other the new converts out of them, to be imprisoned, persecuted, and slain; and so the brother would deliver up the brother to death, and the father the child, and the children would rise up against their parents, and a man's foes be they of his own household. Such was the prophecy in this tenth chapter, and such the graphic history which fills it up. "Not peace, but a sword." Though not in a literal sense, yet in a secondary and spiritual sense, these words apply undoubtedly to Christ and Christianity. The sword of the Spirit is mightier than all earthly weapons; and this by no means does our Saviour renounce or lay aside. His religion was to be aggressive and uncompromising beyond all others. He would accept no niche in the heathen Pantheon, merely to be tolerated there. He meant to overthrow all the idols of the time, and sweep them clean away, and reign Himself alone. He might have avoided all persecution by compromise, or by withdrawing from the conflict, as the Essenes did, into the mere luxury of private devotion; and then, like the Essene religion, Christianity would soon have faded from the earth, and humanity would have groaned under its burden forever. But, no. His disciples went forth in the battle against wrong, to conquer and slay it, and hold their lives cheap in the conflict; and no friendships were to hinder the loyalty of the disciple to Christ and his doctrine. "He that loveth father or mother more than me is not worthy of me; and he that loveth son or daughter more than me is not worthy of me." Such is the spiritual meaning. "Not peace, but a sword."

There are some practical lessons which come from the subject, which I want to draw out and apply.

And the first pertains to the true relation and bearing of the Church of Christ to the unbeliefs and evils of the time. Two courses or methods are recommended. One is to make peace with the world, to compromise with it; to sheathe the sword of the Spirit, and give over the conflict between Christianity and unbelief, and concede that nothing beyond this present life is known with sufficient certainty to warrant any dispute about it. As we were taught the other day, by one who occupies a Christian pulpit, we might draw the atheist into our Christian communions by saying to him, "We have the same difficulties that you have; we are only inquirers about this matter: come join us, and inquire with us. This is the true liberality in religion, to do away with all creeds, since one is as good as another, and none are of any authenticity or value." And so a missionary at the West, who went to establish a society where there were known to be philosophical unbelievers, left out from his published articles the idea of God, in the hope of winning their confidence and co-operation. And what is the answer which the world makes to this policy? It is this: "If you Christians have inquired eighteen hundred years on these subjects, without coming to any conclusions, you are not the people for us to go to school to; much less if, having reached conclusions, you are afraid to announce them and stand by them as the strength and inspiration of your moral manhood." Infidelity is bold enough and honest enough in its denials; and it will have only contempt for any form of religion which tries to split the difference between yes and no.

So, then, the other method is affirmation, aggression, and conflict of good with evil, and truth with error, where the sword of the Spirit flashes with its sharpest and clearest splendors. Christianity is aggressive, or it is nothing. The Church is militant, or it goes under; for the grand truths it holds — of the Divine Personality, of immortality, of the spiritual nature of man, of his probation here, of his moral responsibilities which hold him to endless retributions, of his origin, dignity, and worth, as the heir of an endless life — are in sharp contrast with the negations of unbelief which make him only a creature of this world, to be extinguished in it at last. So that still the motto is, "Not peace, but a sword." And there is another lesson. Observe, the great virtues come into exercise only by moral conflict and spiritual warfare. In a dead and sleepy uniformity, the reason is benumbed and dwarfed, and there is room only for cowardice, and torpor of both mind and heart, and indolence and indifference to all truth; and that is spiritual death. In conflict there is the enlargement of the reason, and the waking-up of all the faculties, and full scope for candor and magnanimity and enlightened tolerance, and the sweet charities which come from a profounder knowledge of the wants, the weaknesses, and the fallibilities of human nature. A little Christianity, or a false one, will not cure the native conceit and arrogance of the human heart; and all bitterness and bigotry come not of religion, but the want of it. They are the virus of the natural man, that needs to be purged away. For that reason, Christ is to be preached, and his truth made aggressive; for, the nearer you come to the heart of Christ, so much the more will you be clothed in his gentleness and grace, and so much more of the heavenly temper will be transfused through the battle of right with wrong. Christianity is the most liberal where there is the most of it; because there we learn the worth of human souls, and the dangers that beset them, and are brought into full commiseration with all their wants and woes; and because there, if anywhere, our pride and arrogance are taken out of us, and all personal exaltation is rebuked as we affirm closes over them, because the flaming sword of the Spirit has never been drawn! The kingdom of God is within you, if you ever attain it; and it comes not by compromise, but it comes by power. So Jesus conquered before ever He tried to conquer the world. His first conflict was in that forty days' battle with temptation; and not till the end of it, came the peace within from the overshadowing wings of the ministering angels. We must follow Him to the same heights of peace, if we ever reach them, for there is no roundabout way; and we shall not be borne to them on beds of ease, nor on the tides of our passions. We fight our way, or we never get there. And only from the heights won by conquest can we take up the song of victory, —

> Lo, the pathway lies behind us,
>    Where we marched o'er heaps of slain;
> Where our vanquished foes lie bleeding,
>    All along the battle-plain:
> All the sordid troop of Mammon,
>    Coward Fear, and Lust of Praise,
> Death that cast his baleful shadow
>    Over all our darkling ways, —

> Unbelief that feeds on ashes,
>    Fear of man that brings a snare,
> Selfish Grief, and selfish Pleasure,
>    Carnal Pride, and haggard Care,

> Satan in fair form transfigured,
>   Strewing garlands on the road,
> To install our vaunting Reason
>   On the eternal throne of God.

Such are the enemies in this conflict of Christ with the world; and, these everywhere overcome, the song over Bethlehem floats over the whole world, " Peace on earth, and good-will amongst men."

the great verities of the gospel. Liberality or comprehension or Broad Church is not the aggregation of all sorts of opinions and things, but the vital belief and practice of those which bring you into most loving fellowship with all humanity and consecration to its welfare; and it demands just as well the rejection of those that would dash down its hopes of regeneration and progress. Christ Himself *denounced* only hypocrisy and wrong. To these his words were forked lightnings. To simple benighted unbelief, to mere errors of creed or errors of practice, his warfare was like the conflict of the dawn with the darkness; and his prayer, "Father, forgive them." None so comprehending as He; and none whose doctrine discriminated more sharply the truth that cleanses and inspires human nature, from the falsities that darken and lead astray. For the sake of humanity, then, for the sake of charity, for the sake of that love of man which has all the gall of the natural heart purged out of it, and all the tenderness of God breathed into it, — not peace, but a sword, for the falsities that hinder the reign of Christ on earth and in the human soul.

And there is another lesson still. For the sake of peace itself, that peace which is profound and real, and not a patched-up truce with evil and wrong, Jesus brings first the sword of the Spirit. There are two kinds of peace. There is the peace that comes by compromise with evil, and there is the peace that comes by conquest over evil. The first is a hollow truce: the last is the peace of God that passeth understanding. The first comes from moral weakness: the last is peace by power. Look into your own heart or your own experience, if you are a Christian man or woman, and you will have a perfect representation of the way in which the kingdom of God comes on. It comes by conquest, if it comes at all. You cannot lie down and sleep, and let the evils in you have their own way, — the lust of the flesh, the lust of the eye, and the pride of life, the love of self and the love of the world and the love of ease, the doubts and the fears which are born of unbelief, or the passions the angers and the hatreds that are born of sin. You cannot make peace with all these. No, you must grapple with them, and slay them, and have them under your feet; and then comes peace, full of joy, as Channing says, without one throb of tumultuous passion, the prelude of the peace of a happier world. This is the peace by power. The conflict may be long and arduous; but this is the auspicuous consummation. And this we always pray for in the words, "Thy kingdom come." It is the battle of life within you every day, — the battle between the world with its encroaching line of conquest, and the kingdom of God which comes on to take possession. One recedes as the other advances; and, alas! how many go down under the god of this world, and its wave of conquest

# THE ATONEMENT.

JOHN I. 29: "Behold the Lamb of God, that taketh away the sin of the world."

THE Christian atonement is undoubtedly the central doctrine of the New Testament, — say rather of the Old and the New Testament both, — and of all religion which is worthy of the name. Very unfortunately, it has been made the topic of dispute and controversy, though that were to be expected; for what touches the supreme interest of men must needs be a matter of inquiry, and therefore of debate. It is only on one side, however, that there is any room for debate among those who receive the New Testament as a rule of faith. As a subject of philosophy and speculation, involving the reasons of the Divine Government, the subject branches off into the unknown and the unknowable. Brought home to us in its practical bearing, it is so plain that the wayfaring man, though a fool, cannot miss the message which the gospel brings.

Have you never noticed, on reading your Bibles, that indescribable tone of *concern* with which always the Divine message comes to men? Even if we could not distinctly articulate the doctrines of the gospel, we should know by this tone of grieving mercy that something very great was at stake; that the Divine Mind looked into gulfs of ruin too deep for us to fathom, and saw heights of bliss and glory towering beyond our sight; and that there was, if I may so say, the deep anxiety of the Divine Mind to save men from the one, and raise them up into the fruition of the other. This *tone* of the message, quite as much as the matter of it, is what searches us and finds us when reading our Bibles; and it gives unction to that deep and tender pathos which breathes through the discourses of Jesus, as in the farewell to Jerusalem: —

"How often would I have gathered thy children as a bird gathers her brood under her wings!"

The atonement is oneness with God, — man reconciled. Its consummation is described by Jesus, "That they all may be one, as thou, Father, art in me, and I in thee; that they may be one in us, and that the world may believe that thou hast sent me."

1. Christ as a sacrifice;
2. What that sacrifice means and represents;
3. And what conditions it requires of us, — these three topics will unfold the subject, and bring it home to us.

1. "Behold the Lamb of God, that taketh away the

sin of the world." The image is a very expressive and a very beautiful one. A lamb was an offering for sin, — a sacrifice slain for its expiation. Hence Jesus is called the Lamb of God, at the opening of John's Gospel, where, in his first revealing Divine gracefulness, He appears before the evangelist, and the Baptist says, "Here is the Lamb, the sacrifice that is to take away the sin of the world."

And it tones the discourses of Jesus and the New Testament throughout. Jesus is the first Reformer we read of who, at the beginning, took his own death into his plan, as if he knew the plan were a failure if that were left out. Hence the indescribable pathos that swells through his discourses. It is not despondency nor complaint, but that Divine sympathy that tinges every thing with the thought of sacrifice. His body is broken bread, his blood is flowing wine, and the oil that balmed his weary feet was balming them for burial. All through the fourth Gospel we never lose sight of the Son of God as the Lamb that was to be slain.

But let us not mistake. It is not merely the death on the cross that makes Him a sacrifice for man, and cleanses man from sin. By dwelling too grossly on his physical agonies, we may even lose sight of the great truth itself. There was suffering of another kind. The burden of suffering and woe which lay upon a sinful world was all laid upon Him. If you would know what that is, think, some of you, of your own experience. Have you watched at a friend's side, and found every throb of anguish which he felt going through you? Have you found as parent, or brother, or sister, that the woes of your own domestic circle and society were drawn up into your own heart, and were constantly rending its finest strings and tendrils? Then you will have some conception of the sufferings of Him whose family was the whole race of man; who was clothed in our humanity, complete and full-orbed; whose strings and tendrils clasped every child of sorrow; who drew all human suffering up into Himself, and bore it upon his feeling as a burden to be removed. Yea, to get a full conception of Christ as the Lamb of God, we must remember that He stood on a height where all the future lay open before Him, so that the woes and sufferings, not of the time then present, but of our humanity down all that opening future, were to Him a present reality, and lay as a present burden upon his soul. It was not the sins of men *imputed* to Him. No! It was sin, in its nature and its results, lying as a burden on the race of man, through the whole of which he felt the drawings of the ties of brotherhood, and which He drew up into his great Divine Heart till it broke under a weight too heavy to be borne. Hence you see the burden of meaning in the words, "God laid on Him the iniquities of

Do not say that this is a questioning of the Divine Perfections. The Divine Nature were not perfect if it were only stone and ice, like the natures of some men, that never melt and flow in drops of mercy. It is the very height of its perfection that brings out of the Divine Fatherhood a daily sacrifice for the sin of the world, and hence imaged forth in time by the Lamb of God, made a whole offering for human redemption.

Such, then, is the Christ as a sacrifice; and such is the truth which the sacrifice represents, leading us upward into the wealth of the Divine Nature itself, and the very heart of the Divine Mercy.

3. But we come to our third and practical point, where the subject bears directly upon us, and comes home to each one of us. What conditions does this sacrifice require of us?

It requires faith, — faith in Christ as the Lamb of God, and faith in that eternal and costly sacrifice which is imaged forth, as a condition of seeing ourselves as we are, and of seeing the nature and consequence of all our disobedience. Not till we see the burden of our sin lying heavy on the Divine Heart, are we brought to any thing worthy the name of repentance, or to any real atonement and reconciliation with God, — not till we see every sin of ours as a stab at the Divine Feeling itself.

There was a man given over to debauchery and

sin, from whose mind and heart the threatenings of the law and the thunders of the pulpit had for years rebounded as from casings of iron. But at length, in the depths of his sin, the Holy Spirit reached him in a form that arrested and held him. A light not of earth seemed falling around his feet. He looked up, and he saw a Divine Sufferer on his cross, though that cross sent out radiations of glory; and a voice fell down upon his ear, "Have I suffered all this for you, and is that the return you make?" And the man whom threatenings had never reached found his whole nature melted down in penitence, and fluid in the Divine Hand, and run anew in heavenly moulds. And the impenitent unbeliever went forth with a heart throbbing with the love of Christ and the love of man, and with a faith tongued with celestial fire. He became one of the flaming heralds of the Cross. Vision, do you say? — morbid imagination? But morbid imaginations never change men from morbid iniquity to moral health and a new heavenly life; whereas the Spirit of God, all-searching and all adaptive, does reach men in forms and representations suited best to their cases, and suited best to bear in the Sovereign Grace upon the soul.

What, then, are the conditions which the Divine Sacrifice requires of us? Faith, — faith in God, not as a mere abstraction, not as a sovereign who only threatens you with the punishment of hell, but as a us," — yours and mine, and those of every member of this great brotherhood of mankind. The sufferings of the cross were for Him of only six hours' duration, whereas in most cases they were a prolonged agony of days and weeks. In the case of our Saviour, the sufferings were short, because the agony of heart and mind had already been so great and prolonged, that the physical life was well-nigh drained to its very dregs. Such was the Lamb of God made an offering for sin, to take away the guilt of the world.

2. But this truth leads us to another and a higher one. Jesus as the Christ is the expression of the Divine Nature, — the Divine Fatherhood, in fact, brought nigh to man, and openly revealed. Here, as nowhere else, is the Divine Personality made manifest, the only begotten Son who dwells in the bosom of the Father, and brings Him forth to view. Hence the sufferings of Christ image forth to us the Divine sufferings for the sins of men. Compassion! Sympathy! How coldly do men talk of the Fatherhood of God, and then proceed straightway to discharge the doctrine of all significance! as if He dwelt apart, and looked from a distance upon the sins and sufferings of men, perhaps sending prophets to them to denounce punishment, or promise pardon on repentance. The cross! Why, it symbolizes the truth that God bears a cross in his own feeling, that there is a wounding and a bleeding of the Divine Love with

every rejection of its pleadings and every sin. And hence we find that this image of sacrifice and suffering is carried up to the Divine Nature itself. And so the same evangelist, when the heavens were opened to him, and God was revealed as Divinely Human, saw in the midst of the throne a Lamb as it had been slain. Nobody takes this in the letter, or believes that the Divine Nature can suffer physically; but to believe that God is a person and not an insensate force, and that the Father is imaged forth in the Son, is to believe also that the Divine Affection can and must draw up into itself the griefs and sufferings of our entire humanity.

God as revealed in the Christ is a Father in the midst of his family. What would you think of an earthly father who saw his family dying around him, dying, too, by their own fault and their own guiltiness, and yet did not suffer with them in heart, mind, and soul; yea, whose life-chords did not run down through all their griefs, and draw them up into his own nature, as on electric wires? And such is God in his Fatherhood; not away off in the heavens, but immanent in all our affairs, hidden close beneath our consciousness, present by a more still and inaudible pulsation in every beating of our hearts, taking into his own feeling the anguish that pierces ours; and so his own Divine Nature, that suffers with ours, is imaged in the Lamb slain from the foundation of the world.

Being whose love you wound, and whose mercy you grieve, with every act of disobedience. Never does a man see his sins in their true character till he sees them so opposed to the Divine Nature that in every one of them his Lord is crucified anew. Never will the wrong done to his brother appear to him in its true light till he looks up, and sees a Divine Sufferer who says to him, " Because you have done it unto him, you have done it unto me." Never is repentance any thing but a selfish fright and fear of punishment, never is reformation any thing but an outward conformity, till we look up, and see through our tears the Lamb in the midst of the throne. Never is the Divine Mercy any thing to us but a cold proclamation of pardon, till we receive it as a Mercy which has bled under wounds that we have inflicted. But, when it is thus received, we enter into the heart of it; and the sense of forgiveness is indescribably profound and tender; and we enter into the Divine meaning, " Behold the Lamb of God, that taketh away the sin of the world."

And only then do we enter into such communion with God, and become so far forth partakers of his nature, that our faith in Him gives us the heart of flesh, and the morality and charity that are filled with the throbbings of his love. Paul worshipped God as a Sovereign, after the straitest and most rigid of rituals; and he was very much like the God he worshipped, hard and unrelenting. But he met, one day, one who appeared out of the bending heavens, and told him, "I am Jesus, whom thou persecutest: I am the one you are slaying." And the flint all melted out of him; and he became full of the spirit of the Lamb of God, and tender-hearted as a child. So only God takes your sins away. His promises may bribe you into virtue, his punishments may keep you from sinning with your hands; but only through the Lamb of God He will take away your sins, melt them clean out of you, and make your souls beat with the throbbings of his own Divine Humanity.

Has Christianity come to any of you only as a code of rules and regulations, without laying a warm hand upon your spiritual natures to mould them anew? Has sin appeared to you only as an inconvenience, or as a violation of social customs and manners? Has the religion of Christ failed to stir your deepest affections, and to move you to a consecration to Him, fervent and complete; failed of giving you the sense of forgiveness and peace that flows in like a river, clear and tranquil? That must be, and will be, unless the doctrine of the Fatherhood is something more than an empty platitude, and unless his Christ, as the Lamb of God, shall take your sins away.

# THE TRINITY.

MATTHEW XXVIII. 19: "Go ye therefore, and teach all nations, baptizing them in the name of the Father, and of the Son, and of the Holy Ghost."

1 JOHN, V. 7: "There are three that bear record in heaven: the Father, the Word, and the Holy Ghost; and these three are one."

THIS text from the first Epistle of John has a remarkable history. A very long controversy has been held over it; not merely as to what it means, but as to whether it has any rightful place in Sacred Scriptures. The final verdict by all parties is, that it is a spurious text, since it is not found in any of the early manuscripts which have any authority. It does not follow, however, that it is a forgery; and it is hard to believe it such. It came into the Bible, I suppose, in this way: Some early copyist put it in the margin, as a comment, or note upon the text, meaning it as a paraphrase and enlargement of what the text had only hinted and implied. Another copyist came along, and removed it from the margin into the text itself, and embodied it there, thinking, perhaps, that it belonged there originally, and had fallen out, and ought to be restored. And, if you read over the whole passage, you will see that it does give to the sense a roundness and completeness which you miss, and see the want of, when it is taken away. No doctrine of Christianity is affected by it; for these three terms are found elsewhere, in like connection and relation, — Father, Son, and Spirit, as expressing the entire nature of the Godhead. I regard therefore the text in John as an early gloss or commentary, probably suggested by the text in Matthew, and serving as an illustration. For, observe how beautifully the one illustrates and complements the other. Matthew reports Jesus as saying to his disciples, "Go and teach all peoples," so I render it, "baptizing [i.e., cleansing] them by the power of the Father and the Son and the Holy Ghost. And lo, I am with you alway, to the end of time." But lest any one should fall into the mistake of thinking that these were three persons, or three Gods, the text in John says they are three forms of attestation of one God: "There are three that bear witness in heaven: the Father, the Word, and the Holy Ghost; and these three are one;" so giving us the conception of the Godhead in his undivided personality.

But a subject of most profound interest here opens upon us. This meaning certainly unfolds itself from both passages, that, in order to have any living experience of the wealth of the Divine Nature, you must know God in a threefold sense. You must know

Him as Father, Son, and Holy Ghost. Nay, you have no baptism, no unction from Him, no inward cleansing, — for that is what baptism signifies, — unless you know Him in his threefold power as Father, Son, and Spirit. How constantly do we find this truth brought out all through the New Testament! It is not enough, Christ tells us, to believe in the Father. "He that believeth not on the Son shall not see life; but the wrath of God abideth on him." Nor yet, again, is this enough. "I will send the Comforter," He says, sometimes rendered Helper. "He shall convict, convince, bring all I have spoken to your remembrance, take of mine and show it to you, and show you things to come." What, then, are these three grand essentials of the gospel, without all of which our Christian experience is lame, halting, and defective, but all of which together reveal the Godhead in the fulness of his perfections and the riches of his grace? Let us give our attention to them severally.

1. When we speak of God as our Father, we mean specially God as the universal, all-begetting, and omnipotent Love. It is not by any means a word which exhausts the full meaning of Deity, or the full power and manifestation of the Godhead. Indeed, there is no single term that will do this. "Fatherhood" is a word borrowed from our human relations, which, however, very feebly represent it. It is the all-

originating Love which not only created us at the beginning, but which creates us all the while, and which is transfused through all the works of Nature; is within all Nature's laws, and working through them. It knows nothing of persons. In good men or bad men, it works on just the same. Hence our Saviour's language, " Love your enemies, bless them that curse you, do good to them that hate you, and pray for them that despitefully use you; that you may be children of your Father which is in heaven: for He maketh his sun to rise on the evil and on the good, and sendeth his rain on the just and on the unjust." Hence, again, He tells the Jews, when they charged Him with working miracles on the Sabbath, "My Father worketh continuously, and so do I." He keeps on Sabbath days just the same. The sun does not then stop shining, nor the grass stop growing, nor the flowers stop blooming. And you may go out under the open heavens, amid the universal tranquillity. If you do any deed of darkness there, or speak out words of blasphemy, the sun will not stop shining, nor the earth stop blooming, nor the breezes stop whispering, nor will any thunderbolt drop down upon your head. Say what you will, do what you will, the omnipresent Love answers back to you in smiles. The Fatherhood of God is that which Wordsworth drank in and described: —

> "Whose dwelling is the light of setting suns,
> And the round ocean, and the breathing air,
> And the blue sky, and in the mind of man;
> A motion and a spirit which impels
> All thinking things, all objects of all thought,
> And rolls through all things."

Or, as Paul puts it, "It is above all, and through all, and in you all;" and, "all in all."

And hence the Fatherhood of God is not specially a Christian doctrine. Long before Christ came, the Greeks called God the universal Father; and the Romans copied them and followed them, for Jupiter means God the Father, all-embracing, all-pervading, like the ethers which we breathe. No people were ever more keenly alive than the Greeks to the omnipresent Love which originated Nature, and which so breathes through it as to make the Cosmos musical in its harmonies, and tremulous in its spirit of beauty.

Well, why is not this enough, and what do we want more? Why, it is enough for a while, and so long as the surface of our natures only, and the surface of universal nature, has come to our knowledge. But, in some hour of self-revelation, the soul within you has been stirred to its depths, and cries out for a personal communion and a personal love, such as no human love can satisfy, and such as nature has not given you. You go out and seek for this communion with the universal Father. You pray into universal space; and your voice comes back in lonely echoes, or in the whispering breeze, which whispers just the same whether you pray or not. Or, there is the burden of sin and guiltiness that lies hard and heavy upon the spirit; you want it rolled off; and you pray to the universal Father to clear it away, and to bring into the wounded mind a sense of forgiveness, atonement, and peace. And still the prayer goes up, and comes back in echoes, —

> "I cannot find Thee: still on restless pinion
>   My spirit beats the void where Thou dost dwell;
> I wander lost through all thy vast dominion,
>   And shrink beneath thy light ineffable."

"I cannot find Thee." Or, again, some friend has been stricken at your side, — some one whose heart was so knit with yours that they both made but one heart, — and he passes away from your sight, and dissolves back into universal nature; and you plant withering flowers above him, to represent too well the human flower that turns to dust below. And you try to follow his spirit where it vanished away in the dark. You knock at the gates of death; but they give back only a hollow sound. You shout through them after your friend; but there is no answer except your own voice coming back again. What, then, do you want? What do the heart and mind both cry out for? Why, it is the Word, the *Word*, the WORD.

Not your own word given back to you, not the inarticulate word of star and breeze, not any man's word that is fallible, not a mere voice of command as from Sinai. It is the Word begotten of the Father, and coming in tones more human and determinate than the tones of Nature, more human than her breezes or her thunders. It is *the Word made flesh*, fresh out of the bosom of the Godhead, clothed in our humanity, and speaking its language, and breathing its sympathies, and warm and tender with its tones. "No man hath seen God at any time: the only begotten Son that dwells in the bosom of the Father, He hath brought Him out to view." The Word doubtless is in Nature also; but there it has no human tones nor sympathies, and no articulation. In the Word made flesh, God is not only humanized to our conceptions, but He speaks with us as a man talks with his friend. "He that hath seen me hath seen the Father; and how sayest thou, then, Show us the Father? Believest thou not that I am in the Father, and the Father in me? The words that I speak unto you, I speak not of myself; but the Father that dwelleth in me, He doeth the works." To the question, Where have the loved ones gone? not only comes back an articulate answer, but the bolts and bars are broken by Him who went through and shattered them. Not only so: God Himself, not in material Nature, whose pulses have no blood in them, but in humanity all divine and lovable, and thrilling towards us with tender compassion, and taking up all our sufferings as a burden on its own feeling, — all this comes in the Word made flesh, appealing to the deepest love of the heart, and seeking personal relations with every one of us. We appeal from nature to the Word, with a new song upon our lips.

> On surface knowledge we have fed,
>   And missed the golden grain;
> And now I come to Thee for bread
>   To sate this hunger pain.
>
> No gift I bring, nor knowledge fine,
>   Nor trophies of my own:
> I come to lay my heart in Thine,
>   O Lamb amid the throne!

There is unquestionably a dispensation of *law*, in which we are governed by principles, ideas, and codes of morality. And all this we may have with only an acknowledgment of the Fatherhood of God. It is a dispensation of truth; and it may have a good deal of truth, even all the abstract truths of religion, and yet never touch the deep well-springs of human nature. Indeed, I do not know that there was any abstract religious truth that had not been acknowledged long before Christ came. The Fatherhood of God, immortality as a speculation, retribution, heaven and hell, and the whole moral code, were not the discoveries of Christianity, but were given in some shape by all the great religions of the East. The principles of absolute morality are the same, all the world over, and all the ages through. But an abstract code of morals, of doctrine, commands without inspiring. Laws may be good and beneficent, yet command without inspiring. Natural law is all good; and the naturalist tells us how divine it is working around us and through us. I see all this, and acknowledge it. I see, too, that the regulations of a railroad may be very good and wise and beneficent; and I know very well, that, unless I keep within those regulations, I shall very likely be maimed, or crushed to death. And I may believe that the railroad directors, whom I have never seen, and who hold their sessions away off in some committee-room, are very wise and good people. And I shall observe the regulations in a mechanical way, without being brought into any relations with the directors, that edify me much, intent only on getting to my journey's end. And so it is in our great journey of life, while we have only a code of natural and moral laws, whose Lawgiver is away out of sight, and keeps this stupendous mechanism in motion. And we read of a man who was rigidly and fiercely conscientious, while the truths that ruled him were ideas only, categories of the understanding, commandments graven on tables of stone, or drawn out in a Levitical code.

But afterwards the ideas and the categories and the commandments were gathered, embodied, and impersonated in a living Form and the attributes of a Divine Person who broke on his sight, and whose Divine splendors and heavenly communings melted all the iron out of him, and made his heart the well-spring of a philanthropy tender as a mother's love. It made all the difference between Saul of Tarsus with his hardness of character, and Paul to the Gentiles with these touches of softness.

> All that the Father hath is thine;
> Thus does thy Word declare:
> So the full stream of life Divine
> Flows from the Godhead there.

3. Well, why is not this enough? Why is not the love of Christ all-sufficient, — Christ as the manifestation of the Godhead, and a revelation of the Great Hereafter? Because that love may be a sentiment only, and it may be nothing but a sentimentality. Jesus as a lovely character may be admired and extolled as all-Divine; and yet, if that be all, we only admire Him as we do the beautiful nature that smiles around us. And bad men have paid their homage to both, with heart and character unchanged. "I know men," said the first Napoleon; "and I know Christ was something more." But if he did know it, that knowledge did not prevent his wading through

slaughter to a throne. And we may know Christ as a model of perfection and of moral beauty; and the model may only shine away before us, and above us, without melting down our natures and moulding them anew. "The Holy Spirit," said Jesus to his disciples, "is with you, and shall be in you." He was with them, for they saw the Holy Spirit manifest in his person and works; but as yet He was an outside wonder and mystery, and only when Jesus went away, and came again, did they know the nature of his kingdom, or even understand his words. When there is not only admiration of his character, but submission to Him of the will and of the life, with a child's obedience and trust, then the Holy Spirit comes. It comes as an influx of power, a forthgoing energy from God, in his Christ and through Him, searching all the man within, making his sins stand black in the light, and in awful contrast with the Divine Purity and Holiness. The Holy Spirit is not a sentiment, but a searcher and refiner, melting the heart into penitence first, and then purging its guilt away. Not only so. He quickens the whole spiritual nature, makes the memory deliver up the dead truths that were in it, and makes them alive. He is the Comforter; for through Him comes all the communion with Christ that we can ever have. The Second Advent people tell us that Christ is coming again in person, and that we shall see Him in the flesh very soon.  As if that would bring Him any nearer to us spiritually, merely looking upon his form, and gazing upon his person.  Only as He sends the Holy Spirit, does He become the Christ of consciousness, convincing, subduing, purifying, and regenerating, and then flooding the soul with his rivers of peace.

Not all people have this that believe in Christ. No; for they may believe in Him only as a lovely model, and admire Him as they admire pictures and statues.  There is a great deal of this artistic religion, which changes one's intellectual tastes without changing the heart, character, and life.  Not till the Word comes in the voice of command and authority, and you fall under it, saying, "Lord, what wilt Thou have me to do?" not till then are you in any state to receive its influx of power, that explores you, sifts your pride and conceit out of you, and creates you anew in Christ Jesus.  Then the Holy Ghost comes in showers of arrowy light, first piercing and wounding, and then changing to showers of forgiving grace and abounding love.  Then He comes in power, and gives his people pentecostal times.  But He strives with us all the while.  I think all of you must have known something of his motions within you.  Can you not remember an hour when the conscience was more tender, or some neglected truth was pricking at the core of the heart, or the unrest and dissatisfaction with mere selfish and godless living were more intolerable, or when your violations of the law of neighborly love hindered you from sleep, or when the cravings of unsatisfied affection made a fearful void in the soul, or when vanished smiles and household voices hushed in death have made the silence as that which follows the toll of bells, tolling through the heart forever, or when a coming eternity, coming so nigh, has folded you in the shadows which it sends on before, and the questions, Whence? and Whither? have been sharp and urgent? If you can remember such hours as these, then the Spirit has had its strivings with the conscience. And *self-surrender* is the sole condition of his coming with power, till the troubled mind and heart find their eternal peace under the brooding wings of the Holy Dove.

Such is the Christian Trinity, — Father, Son, and Spirit, — clear of all husks of theology which we ought by this time to have done with, in quest of the golden grain which lies within them. And if we are to know the Father, not as a speculation, but as a personal friend; if we would know Christ, not as a barren sentiment, but as the transforming Word; if we are to know God as a living experience that opens through the soul all the riches of his nature, — we must have a baptism into the power of the Father, and the Son, and the Spirit, — all three; and then the promise of Christ will have its blissful fulfilment, " Lo, I am with you alway, even unto the end of the world." "If any man love me, he will keep my words: and my Father will love him, and we will come and make our abode with him."

# THE DIVINE FRIENDSHIPS.

JOHN XI. 35, 36: "Jesus wept. Then said the Jews, Behold how He loved him!"

TWO ranges of fact appear in the life of Jesus, seeming, at first, altogether discrete and separate. One range is called miracle, or wonder. Events of this class appear at first like solitary peaks, very lofty, and mingling with the sky; and on them Jesus is lifted away from us, away from all our home-life and every-day experience. Hence it is the peculiarity of one school of criticism to take all this range out from the New Testament history, as unreal and unhistoric, and belonging only to the category of myth and fable. The birth of Jesus; his power over diseases; over the elements, such as storms and waves; over the dead, who rise to life again at his word; over the grave itself, which had no power to retain Him, — these are taken out as being fabulous and unreal, and the additions of a later age. However, as these exceptional facts are examined and more familiarly apprehended, we find they have this most remarkable peculiarity: they cease to be exceptional, or to stand forth as isolated history. They are woven in with other facts and other history; with the home-life of Palestine, by threads so fine and so tender, that, if you take them out, you draw every thing along with them, yea, whole tracts and provinces of experience which are abloom with the sweetest every-day virtues, and filled with the very fragrance of social and domestic love; and you find there is no Christ left, and no history left, but in the place thereof only a gaping vacuity for the Christian ages to date from. When you stand here, and look off through a clear atmosphere, you see Wachuset and Monadnock, and their brother hills, standing blue against the sky. Some child, perhaps, would think they are not mountains at all, but only clouds that hang in air. But travel on towards them, and you pass through green fields, crops of grain, slopes that rise in gentle gradation; the blue tinge fades out, and in place thereof there is waving and fluttering foliage; and when you get to the top you cannot tell where the mountain began, and where the plain ended, with such gentle undulations does it trend off into smaller hills, and the smaller hills into the plains and valleys.

Now, it is just so with those events in the life of Jesus which we call his "mighty works." They are made up of a great many works, because so much of our common life runs into them, and fills them out with the sweetness of humanity. He healed the sick; but how did He heal them? Why, by drawing them up into the great heart of his love, and thence sending thrills of life into them that went down into their physical frames, and made even the cripple to leap for joy. He raised the dead; but how did He raise them? Why, by holding the immortal spirit within his own Divine sympathies, so that the body, which had been the spirit's dwelling-place, found its frozen currents to melt and start anew, as the warmed and invigorated spirit revived within it. Hence you find that it was not power exercised arbitrarily, but power threaded with the finest nerves of sensibility; as when we are told He raised the young man, the only son of his mother, and she a widow, He helped him from the bier, and handed him to his mother, making the miracle more significant in the manner of it than the mere fact of it, by those Divine courtesies which were fragrant with his benignity and grace.

There is a notion about the miracles of Christ which make them not his works, but arbitrary interpositions of God's power, something adjoined to Him as proofs of the truth He was to utter; as if He should say, "See! I am going to announce a great truth, and to show you that it comes from God. See how I can heal this cripple; or see how I can still the waves; or see how I can raise this dead man to life! See how I can do these wonderful things! Do you think that God would have given such physical power as this to a man whose words were not to be credited and received?" I am afraid there is an old Unitarianism which still clings to these mechanical theories of the works of Jesus, because afraid to acknowledge his essential and intrinsic Divinity.

We are going to contemplate this morning the miracle at Bethany not as a mere manifestation of power, but as a revelation of life and character; not as an arbitrary interposition of God, but as the natural and spontaneous forthgoing of the mind and heart of Jesus. And having contemplated the miracle as a revelation of life and character, we will then ascend to the grander and more general doctrines of Christianity, which are shadowed forth, from the resurrection scene at Bethany, to the general resurrection of the last day.

1. First look at the connections and environments, which are a part of the miracle, in fact, and are as full of its spirit as they can hold.

Observe what a whole group of characters stand out individualized and photographed in the light of this central fact of the raising of Lazarus. There are four persons who specially appear in it with marvellous distinctness, and so drawn to the life, that we know the whole scene must be real. These are Lazarus, the two sisters, and Judas Iscariot. We are accustomed so much to speak of the philanthropy of

Jesus, of his mission to the race, that I fear we miss those interior friendships which give us the sweetest shadings of moral beauty, and the gentlest revealings of his Divinity, and so we fail to see what Christianity does for the private and personal relations of human life. Even the first three evangelists understand this very imperfectly; and not till John comes along, and supplements them, do we see Jesus in those Divine friendships into whose spirit John so largely entered. There was a woman, say Mark and Luke rather awkwardly, who came when Jesus and the twelve were reclining at meat, and poured a box of precious ointment over the head of Jesus; and the disciples rebuked the woman for the needless waste. Open John, and compare notes, and you get the real significance of the scene, and the spirit of it. What the woman really did, was to lave the brow of the weary traveller with spice-waters; take off the worn sandals from the lacerated feet, and bathe them with healing oil; and when Judas Iscariot says, "This ought to have been sold for so much, and put into the money-box," Jesus replies, "Let her alone: are the offices of personal affection worth nothing? I tell you it is just such deeds as these — not the splendid donations and charities thrown from a distance — that will give to my religion its sweetest flavor; yea, as the fragrance of this ointment fills the room, they will make Christianity fill the world with its rich and grateful odors." This woman was Mary,— that same Mary who belonged to the family group at Bethany; and the story gives us some conception of those personal ties whereby Jesus drew all into the great heart of his love, and thence sent out from it life-giving streams that flowed into the languid currents of disease or the frozen channels of death, and made them start anew. In what love-light do the sisters and the brother stand out before us! And so we come to the resurrection scene prepared to understand the nature of it.

Bear in mind that Jesus, though twenty-five miles away, had held the dying man to Himself, knew the whole progress of the disease, through the sympathies of his nature that divined the whole. So He says, "Lazarus has gone to sleep, and I am going to wake him up." The scene at the tomb we are hardly let into by the common rendering. "He groaned in spirit," the translators say; rather it is, He struggled with Himself,— He choked down his emotions; and then, with a great voice, He says, "*Lazarus, come forth!*" great, that is, not in its loudness, but in its volume, because of the fulness of the love that rolled through it, and found its response in the spirit of Lazarus muffled there in death-robes, and called back to conscious life. How vividly does this scene let us into that province of life where Christianity has its special application, and from which, sometimes, it is pushed clean out! There is such a thing as philanthropy so universal, that it knows nothing of the fine tendrils of personal affection; benevolence so mighty large, that the friendships of life have no place in it, to keep it sweet and warm; reformers so bent on saving whole races of men, as to become sour and hard towards the individuals that nestle close beside them. Here is a man who felt the salvation of a world lying hard upon him, whose private friendship had such fervency that the dead came to life in the sphere of it; and its perfume has come down the ages as the fragrance of an everlasting rose. Talk about a miracle! Why, a miracle is only the central fact of a whole congeries, all depending on it. It is power made searching and pervading and all-knowing, through the sympathies of the heart. The central fact and the whole beautiful environment depend each on the other, with the veins of truth running through them alike; just as the earth and the rocks, which are the frame-work of the mountain, are one with the verdure that clothes it, or the flowers that crop out from it and festoon its sides.

But we ascend from this exposition to the grand doctrines of Christianity. These resurrection scenes, in which Jesus appears as the central figure, are types and representations of the final resurrection itself. "If I be lifted up," said he, "I will *draw* all men unto me," — mark the language, I will *draw* them. "This is the will of Him that sent me, that every one who seeth the Son, and believeth in Him, may have everlasting life: and I will raise him up at the last day." "I am the Resurrection and the Life: and he that believeth in me, though he were dead, yet shall he live." Sinking the spirit in the letter, the theologians have transferred the final resurrection scene to the cemeteries. I do not see why; for suppose these same bodies are to rise again, they are not in the graveyards, — they have gone into the endless circulations of nature, have been drawn up, and turned into leaf and flower and forest. And why should not the resurrection be in groves and gardens, rather than among the tombs? But suppose such a scene were possible, what would it be? Suppose Jesus were to come into the churchyards to receive the dead, what would be the nature of the resurrection scene? Why, it would not be the Son of man descending in flaming fire. It would be the resurrection scene at Nain or at Bethany over again, extended and enlarged, but the same benignant Form in the midst of it; and his Spirit pervading the whole. It would not be an arbitrary power over dead bodies, but the power of spirit over spirit, and over matter made quick by its power and by its all-healing and searching sympathies. The child would be raised up and handed to the mother, the brother to the sister, the friend to the friend long separated, with, " Loose him, and let him go home to his own." That would be Nain and Bethany over again. And what scenes in all the burial places! What groupings of old friends revived, of families coming together, whose dust had been scattered abroad! What home centres forming themselves anew, circle within circle, as over all the earth, each one rose and came to his own, as doves that fly to their windows! But the scene, which the theologians have imagined as here on earth and in the cemeteries, is beyond the cemeteries, not among dead bodies, but among living souls who have put on immortality.

> "The dear departed that have passed away
> To the still house of death, leaving their own, —
> The gray-haired sire that died in blessing thee,
> Mother or sweet-lipped babe, or she who gave
> Thy home the light and bloom of Paradise, —
> They shall be thine again, when thou shalt pass
> By God's appointment through the shadowy vale,
> To reach the sunlight of the immortal hills."

"I am the resurrection and the life," means plainly, "Mine is the power over kindred spirits to draw them up to me, by the attractions of a friendship which is the mightiest power in the universe."

You whose hearts are the hardest would melt into penitence, if once drawn into the sphere of a friendship like his. It is not less mighty now than it was here on the earth; not less mighty now that the

Son of man is lifted up, and become the Lamb in the midst of the throne, who leads his own in green pastures and beside fountains of living water. And those who have gone down in sin and unbelief may look up from their sepulchres, may still hear his " Come forth ; " " Loose him, and let him go ; " for there was that other Mary, who had gone down into a worse sepulchre than that of Lazarus. But, —

> " In the sky after tempest as shineth the bow,
> In the glance of the sunbeam as melteth the snow,
> He looked on the lost one, her sins were forgiven ;
> And Mary went forth in the beauty of heaven."

# ENCOURAGEMENTS.[1]

HEBREWS XII. 1: "Seeing we are compassed about with so great a cloud of witnesses, let us renounce every weight, and the sin that doth so easily beset us, and let us run with patience the race that is set before us."

WE hear and read a great deal about the trials and the difficulties of the Christian life; and, if we were confined to this line of thought, we should get the impression that the way to heaven was a very rugged and thorny one, and that it was very hard work to be a Christian; and we might imagine that there was truth in the idea which some have, that, if you decline to take the Christian name and confession, you will have indulgences and pleasures, and a sort of freedom which Christians must renounce, and a right to some practices of doubtful morality, without being criticised. I propose to speak this morning of the *encouragements* and *incitements* of the Christian course; and we begin with this figure of the writer to the Hebrews, which represents it. It is drawn from

[1] The manuscript of this sermon bears the date of October, 1874; and it is believed to be the last sermon written and preached by Mr. Sears. The short and incomplete sermon printed with the memorial discourse of Dr. Chandler Robbins was never delivered by its author.

the Greek stadium, or race-course, where the selectest portion of all Greece assembled once in four years, and where picked men of the most perfect physical development tried their skill in running for the prize. They trained themselves for the contest. They laid aside every weight; that is to say, any garments that cumbered the most swift and easy motion. Long rows of spectators lined the stadium on either side, and clapped their hands in acclamation for their favorite hero, when he left others behind him in the race. Even so, — this is the doctrine of the text, — our life here on the earth is a race-course. Birth is the starting-place, and death is the goal; and just beyond sits the judge who awards the prize of victory; and the spectators are the innumerable company who have passed into the heavens, but who bend over us and around us, to cheer us on to victory. The apostle has just enumerated a long train of martyrs, at the head of whom is Jesus, the Mediator of the New Covenant. So august is the humblest Christian life, and so great the prize it wins, that its success sends thrills of acclamation into the heavens themselves. Dropping the figure, and coming to the thought that is under it, — a Christian course has incitements and encouragements which belong to none other; and now let us see what they are.

The grand distinction between a life heartily and confessedly Christian, and one which is not, I take to be this: that the Christian course has its crosses and hardships and trials, so far as they are peculiar to it, at the beginning, and they grow less and less till they disappear. A wordly life, clearly pronounced such, has its crosses and hardships afterwards. They are cumulative, and grow heavier to the last. The Christian, like Bunyan's pilgrim, finds his load growing lighter, till it falls off. The worldling finds his load grow heavier, till it weighs him down, and he falls under it at the last. It is like the two travellers crossing the Alps from opposite sides. The one who starts in the Tuscan vales goes at first through scenery that charms the senses, and under skies of unparalleled softness. All is delightful for a while. But he creeps along the sunny side of the Alps, and the air becomes cold, and the scenery grows barren. He comes to the region of eternal snow, passes over the summit on the cold northern side: the Italian scenery vanishes from sight. He descends without a guide, wanders through drifts, gets chilled, and finally drops, frozen and dead, into the chasm below. So ends his journey.

The other traveller starts fresh and vigorous on the Switzer side, gets to the summit through toil and difficulty, sees new prospects breaking upon him every hour, passes over to the southern side, where the air grows balmier, and the fields grow greener, and finally comes to the region of Tuscan beauty, where nature has lavished all her charms. So ends his journey. And this is the Christian life. It does begin with self-renunciations and self-denials; and these undoubtedly put crosses and restraints on the lusts and passions of the carnal mind. It does begin with giving up self; and this is always hard at first, when it is hearty and complete. It does begin with actual duties and endeavors, which cross our indolence, and love of ease. It does require of us sometimes to stand up for truths which are not popular, and which are even trampled under the feet of the crowds. It does require at first self-watch and self-analysis, and a surrender to the voice of God within, kept clear and audible above all the blandishments of the world, and the noise of the street. It does require of us to climb, and not to drift. It does require of us to gird up all the loins of the mind, and put all its muscles on the strain, to acquire an individual faith which is clear and sufficing, and not a dead tradition of the elders. It does require habits to be formed, — habits of thinking, and habits of praying, and habits of doing. But all this done, habits become a second nature; and the Christian life becomes not an effort and a self-denial, but a spontaneous and eternal joy; and the hills of difficulty smooth out into prospects green and sunny as Tuscan vineyards.

Illustrate this in another way. A Christian life,

heartily consecrated, reproduces itself in others. Take the family relation as an illustration of this. Every family has a sort of unity. As is the head of the family, so will be the spirit that fills the house, and whose silent, pervasive influence impresses and educates all the young life that is in it. It is very seldom that those who grow up in a Christian home, and go out from it, fall into any of the incurable sins and depravities. The Holy Spirit loves most to operate through the church in the house, and mould all its young life. And so the Christian man sees his own spirit reflected back more and more from those who are near about him. The vice and the filial ingratitude which sometimes imbitter the peace of the household, are generally kept away from the faithful Christian home, where the children have been educated for the skies. So that here again the blessings of a Christian course are cumulative. The Christian lives more and more in others the longer he lives; and his path of blessing broadens and brightens to the close. Not so of the life unconsecrated. Not so of a life merely negative and worldly. Not so of mere negative virtues. They have no warmth and piety in them; and they are not creative, in the family or out of it, of the Christian virtues and graces which come back in blessings along the good man's path, which, the longer he lives even in this world, brightens towards the perfect day. Illustrate in another way. The perfect Christian *assurance*, only comes through Christian living. There is an assurance of immortality, and of its peace and communion, not less perfect and secure than the assurance of the scientist pertaining to the facts of nature. But this does not come of itself. Its evidences are cumulative, beginning with those that are external and historical, but supplemented all the while with those that are inward and spiritual; so that the Christian man, as he passes through the probation of this world, comes all the while into the clearer and warmer sunshine of a higher one; and this heavy burden of *doubt, doubt*, grows lighter till it disappears altogether. And then the shadow of death no longer lies upon his path; and all the burdens of life become light as summer air. For in the assurance and foretaste of the life everlasting, what is this little span of life, with all its burdens and cares, and all its short-lived pleasures and satisfactions? Now we can demonstrate intellectually, by syllogistic reasoning, by historical evidence, that there is a God and a Christ, and a spiritual world; and while a man is working out the problem, his understanding will see that the balance is on the positive side. But his conclusions will not stay with him; and when he goes about his business, it will all look like a beautiful dream, transcendent and unreal. So it has always been. The man of the world begins with a child's faith in God, in prayer, in immortality. But this is traditional and imitative. He may confirm it afterwards, intellectually, by reading books, or by thinking out his syllogisms. But the assurance grows less and less, till finally the balance comes down heavy on the negative side; and, as life progresses, the gathering darkness grows heavier and thicker, and sometimes ends in total night. Mr. Hume was a man of pure moral life and serene temper. He began with the child's trust, and ended in the philosopher's doubt of every thing. And there is one passage in his writings, of terrible import; so terrible, that his publishers struck it out of the later editions. "I am appalled," he says, "at the forlorn solitude in which I am placed by my philosophy; and I begin to fancy myself in the most deplorable condition imaginable, environed in the deepest darkness." So it is that the non-Christian life courses through the evening twilight to the perfect night. So it is that the Christian life courses through the morning twilight to the perfect day. For the doctrines of Christianity ripen to a perfect assurance, by a full confession and practice, by working with the Christ, and doing his will, until, through a personal relation, the eternal life is already realized. And these are the incitements and encouragements to the Christian life. But I do not mean the Christian life merely formal, but one which consecrates all our powers of thinking, feeling, doing; and in such wise that we are willing to lose ourselves in the Christ, and the work which He does here on the earth. If you started on the Switzer side, struggling with self, and wrestling with temptation, climbing sometimes up hills of ice, you are sure to gain the summits where the Divine scenery lies soft and sweet upon the soul. And this is what the apostle calls prayer without ceasing. It is when the stages of doubt and denial and temptation and conflict have all been passed and done with, when evil within and without has been resisted and cleared away, and the peace of the Divine reconciliation is perennial, and we know God, not through blind, traditionary belief, but through a living experience; and then we join hands with the elders before the throne, and the sons of God shouting for joy.

# THE SAXON AND THE NORMAN.

# THE SAXON AND THE NORMAN.

THE pride of ancestry is a sentiment which it is quite safe, within certain limits, to indulge. Going back two or three hundred years, you get the history of a class of men who founded churches, states, and empires, and from whom modern civilization borrows almost all its glories. From such men we have descended; and to them most of us, if we take the trouble, can trace a direct and unbroken lineage. Even the humblest individuals, who supposed themselves to be nobodies, will probably find, if they go back far enough, that their line in some of its crossings and counter-crossings runs into that of Howards, Tudors, Stuarts, and Plantagenets; and that the gnarliest fruit that hangs on the most scragged stem of their family-tree has some juices in it which coursed their way through noble branches or from a noble trunk. It will not do, however, to run this up too far. These same lords, prelates, and governors had their ancestors too; and when you come there, if you wish to keep your family pride intact, the best motto on your escutcheon would be, "Oh no, we never mention them!" Through these same nobles and earls, you descended from some sea-pirate or Highland robber; and if he was not hung, the only reason was, that there were not honest people enough to give him his deserts. Such, if you go far enough back, were your ancestors and mine, — grim-looking bandits, lurking in the Cimbric forests, living on plunder, eating horse-flesh raw, and quaffing libations from human skulls. Those of us at the present day who doubt whether the African can be developed into any thing respectable, may well look here, and see out of what they themselves have developed.

This pride of ancestry, however, though liable to its rebuffs and mortifications, may be turned to uses exceedingly valuable, by giving us a living interest in the past. No one knows himself very thoroughly till he sees the stock out of which he sprung. The inborn tastes and proclivities of ancestry course their way downward through all the generations. We vainly suppose that culture and civilization can eradicate them. The innate life of a stock or race of men is as sure to re-appear five, or even ten generations afterwards, as in the one that immediately follows. It is the sap that never loses its flavor, but which enters into the leaves and blossoms of a remote posterity. Those who have the pictures of ancestry hanging on their walls, sometimes observe that the likeness between father and child is not so striking as it is between the child and some ancestral face that looks out from a hoar antiquity three hundred years ago. Hence the study of races not only gives you the clew for understanding the developments of all history, but for understanding yourself, — of tracing the motions of that blood that lifts the valves of your own heart, and makes its currents thrill along all your veins and arteries.

It is sometimes assumed by writers who speak rather loosely, that our civilization is Anglo Saxon. That is one element; but it was not until very recently the ruling element in the institutions of the United States. There are four, — the Anglo-Norman, the Anglo-Saxon, the Celtic, and the African. The Celtic and the African, however, are inferior elements, and under the control of the other two. The Norman and the Saxon struggle for supremacy: the former is more fierce and imperious, and, until quite recently, held the ascendant. New England, with the places it has colonized, is purely Saxon; but, if you go South, the style of government, civilization, manners, social and moral culture, is almost as purely Norman; and the conflict between these two, or between the ideas which they represent, is the prolonged strife of one thousand years. In fact, English history is little else than a record of this conflict; and rightly to discern these two elements, is to get the clew for understanding the strifes, mutations, and prospects of the modern civilized world.

It has been charged against the Lyceum, that it demands what is flashy, superficial, and ludicrous; and that one must not import into a popular lecture solid matter and useful information. But I shall venture on the experiment; and I hope I do not compliment your good sense too much, when I ask your attention, through about half an hour of my lecture, to some groupings of facts, without which no one can understand the philosophy of English and American history. Some of these groupings do not lie within the range of common reading, are not to be found in any English books; but their importance is such, that I promise your attention shall be fully rewarded.

The origin of the Saxon, the fountain of that blood that flows through the veins of New England, and beats through all your hearts to-night, will first claim a moment's attention. It is telling us very little, to say that our ancestors came from England. England is composed of three races, which have never yet mixed their blood together so as to efface the first lines of demarcation. Society in England is made up of three layers, piled one above another, each marking an epoch as distinctly as the rock strata mark each a geological era. Of these three layers, the ancient Briton, or Celtic, lies at the bottom, and makes the lowest class of English population. The

Celts are found throughout England, but they abound most in the western part, — in Cornwall, in Wales, and in Yorkshire; and hence the peculiar dialect of those people. Above the native Briton, is the Saxon, making up the middle class of the people of England, — its mechanics, its smaller landed proprietors, its untitled common people, now pressing upward, and becoming largely represented in the House of Commons. These middle classes belong almost universally to the dissenting churches. Puritanism came from this rank, and settled New England. This class is Saxon through and through, and imbues the English mind with its most distinctive life, and tones it with its broad and clear common sense. Above this, and making the topmost layer, is the aristocracy of England, — its king, its nobility, its titled gentry, and its House of Lords. These are purely Norman, or nearly so, — a people very different in origin, characteristics, manners, customs, temperament, and religion. From this class our Southern States were first colonized. These are not dissenters, but almost uniformly Church of England men. And the conflicts in Church and State have been, to a very great extent, the contest of race with race, or the Saxon against the Norman. What they call the Great Rebellion, when the Parliament rose against the lords, and beheaded the king, and put Cromwell in his place, was simply the Saxon layer upheaving the Norman, and for a while getting topmost, but only to subside again. The conflict between prelacy and Puritanism, prolonged now as the contest between High Churchism and Dissent, is mainly Anglo-Saxon life impinging against Anglo-Norman. And the conflict of our day, between Southern chivalry, so called, and Northern institutions and ideas, or, more properly, Feudalism against Abolitionism, is the same thing over again, — the Cavalier pitted against the Roundhead, or the Norman against the Saxon. I do not say that no other elements enter into these antagonisms, for there are many others. I say such is their origin; and hence their peculiar style and tone; and, without this fact, you lack the key to all modern history, and cannot understand the nature, or calculate the issue, of this conflict of ages.

Having said enough, as I think, to vindicate the importance of my theme, and to show its bearings, let me now go back and lift the veil, and show you the Saxon and the Norman in their native groves, and before the former was developed into the Yankee, and the latter into the Cavalier. We shall see how each compares with the other, and how each bears onward the original proclivities of the stock out of which he comes.

Cast your eye upon the map of Northern Europe, and search out the peninsula of Jutland, comprising now the kingdom of Denmark. In the neck of that peninsula was the land of the Saxons at the time when they first emerge clearly into the light of history. They occupied a territory of about seventy miles in length, and half as many in breadth, stretching along the western shore of the neck of the peninsula. This little strip of land, with three desolate islands off the coast, seems to have been their whole territory from the first to the sixth century. It was less by one-half than the territory of Massachusetts, and was a region of sterility and desolation. The strip along the shore was made up of sandy downs and slimy marshes, which the sea always threatened to invade, and over which the northern winds shrieked with maniac fury. Farther inland was a range of hills covered with forests, whose roar, in the winter blast, answered to the roar of the sea. On these barren islands, and in those gloomy forests, the Saxon worshipped his grim idols, sometimes with the horrid rite of human sacrifice. There he built rude temples and habitations; there, before his bloody altars, he used the skulls of his enemies as his drinking-goblets, and poured out libations to Odin, the All-Father. All the days of the week he named from his gods; and we retain the names yet. Sunday is the sun's day; Monday, the moon's day; Wednesday is Woden's day, and so on. From these desolate abodes he issued forth to ravage and plunder; and in all the southern countries the word Saxon was synonymous with pirate. His name was a terror over all the seas and rivers of the Roman empire, and whereever there was a stream deep enough for his boat to make its way. The more enemies he killed, the more pleased, as he thought, were his gods; and more surely, after death, would he be received into the Valhalla, or the Hall of Odin. His form was noble; his eyes blue; his cheeks fair and florid; his hair was carefully cultivated, and rolled over his shoulders; and a special law was enacted which made it penal to pull the hair of a Saxon. The Romans were astonished at finding so much savage ferocity under such comely exterior. But his character, even in this savage state, had two redeeming traits, the pledges of all his future greatness and glory. One was his indomitable perseverance and energy. The other was his estimate of woman, contrasting most admirably with that of the southern and eastern nations, — all of them enervated by lust or polygamy, and gone down in its pollutions. The Saxon regarded woman as nearest to the Divinity, and made her the priestess of his groves. Woman's virtue was held as Divinity, sacred; and woman's purity was kept whiter than the snows of the northern mountains. If she lost this, she was hunted to death by her own sex with savage ferocity. Here, in fact, was the parent of all his future virtues; and hence it was that the Saxon stock mantled with health and teeming vigor, while the southern nations were stricken with impotence and decay. Even the names of the women were musical in sound, and beautiful in their significance. We find Edith, the blessed gift; Béage, the bracelet; Adeláve, the noble wife; Heabérge, tall as a castle; Wynfreda, the peace of man; Ethélhild, the noble war-goddess; Dudda, the family stem; Golde, the golden; Deorswythe, very dear; Deorwyn, the precious joy.

On those barren islands, what would be the first want of the Saxon? Precisely what it has always been, ladies and gentlemen, — his neighbor's land. About the year 600 he began to go west, — the everlasting propensity of the Yankee. Casting his eye over the narrow sea, into the fertile vales and the gentle slopes of Britain, he thought it a better country than his own. He emigrated, — and for the same reason that a Yankee always emigrates, — for better farms. He overran the island; subdued the native Briton, whom he regarded much as we do the native savage of America; drove him into the west of England, or over into Ireland; took possession of his country; became Christianized, or at least thought he did; and established that state of society whence to this day we derive our maxims of household economy and social justice. The right of woman to hold property, her right to attend the Gémót, or assembly of the people, the right of the widow to her dower, —

these were pure Anglo-Saxon ordinances, at a time when woman in Southern and Oriental nations was degraded into a slave and a thing. The trial by jury, the equal right of inheritance among the children, the Gémót, or assembly of the people, answering to our town-meetings and general court, were composed of both sexes, were Anglo-Saxon institutions, and became the imperishable germs of representative government and republican liberty for all ages. Thus the Saxon subdued the Briton or Celt, and established his ordinances in England; and hence the first and second layers of English life and society, — the Briton or Celt at the bottom, and the Saxon top of him.

The Saxon was to be subdued in turn, and another layer was to be formed above him.

The story of the Anglo-Saxon has been told with tolerable fulness by Sharon Turner. But I do not know of any English history that tells us much about the Norman, which gives us an adequate conception of his origin, his character, and his doings, or which does him full justice as an element in English civilization. And yet we owe to him, in the main, that which flings brilliancy over the English name and annals, that which has given to English art its gorgeousness and grandeur, which has inspired English literature and eloquence with its highest fervor, which has fired the English imagination with Orient splendor, which woke in the Middle Ages the spirit of chivalry and that spirit of old romance which threw the charms of poesy over all the dusty ways of life. The Saxon was intensely practical: his love was for houses and lands, and oxen and sheep and hogs ; and his wit was quick at invention in all things pertaining to the arts of husbandry. The Norman contrived to get all these out of his serfs and slaves, while he listened to the songs and harpings of his skalds and the stories of his saga-men, and cheated life out of its meanness by living in a world of his own magical creations.

Cast your eye again over the map, and trace the limits of ancient Scandinavia, constituting that vast northern peninsula since known as Norway and Sweden. That was the land of the Norman when we first get a clear view of him; that is, from the first to the tenth century. His principal stronghold was the coast of Norway. You are aware that the Scandinavian mountains run nearly the whole length parallel to the coast, their sides covered with lofty pines, their tops gleaming with everlasting snows. The shore is thickly indented with bays and inlets, and off the coast a long row of islands stretches away to the polar sea. Between these islands and the coast, the sea is sucked in fearful eddies and whirlpools, and always makes what Byron calls a hell of waters. This region of cold is not without its charms and its romance. In the long winter nights the northern aurora streams to the stars, and turns midnight into day. This aurora is characterized by Humboldt as the "electric torrents" which always fill the sky overhead with an ocean of surging fire. Summer, though short, comes on without any spring, breaking in full splendor from the bosom of winter, when all things storm into life at once, — to-day a field of snow, to-morrow a carpet of living green.

Norway was divided into twelve little kingdoms, each governed by a jarl, or petty sovereign. There were two classes of population, — those who lived by land, and those who lived by sea; and hence two classes of sovereigns, — land-kings and sea-kings. Under the land-kings were landed proprietors, who were a sort of nobility; and under these were serfs, or slaves, who were attached to the soil, and did all its drudgery, — a state of things very much like that lately existing in the Southern States, or the West India islands. The sea-kings lived upon the sea, and lived by piracy and plunder: they never left the ocean, but always kept in their boats, bending to their oars amid the whirlpools, with gleams of auroral light playing around their icy forms, and glaring down the hell of waters into which they plunged; and it was their boast that they never sought shelter under a roof, and never drained their drinking-horns at a cottage fire. You may well imagine that this mode of life did not make them effeminate. The sea-rovers struck out into the broad ocean, five hundred years before Columbus was born, and as early as the ninth century discovered Iceland and Greenland, and explored the coast of North America and New England, as far as Cape Cod. Attached to each of these land-kings and sea-kings was a skald, or poet-minstrel, who always attended the king in battle, that he might know how to describe it, and magnify the praises of his master. In the long winter nights, and under the auroral sky, the skalds and the saga-men would shorten the hours with lofty-sounding epics and war-songs, and with the long story of the past; so that the Northern land had a rich treasury of song and history handed down by tradition, a great while before a written literature had any existence there.

Depping tells us many curious and marvellous tales about a class of men among these Normans, whose race has not yet become extinct. Every king had a set of persons about him called champions, whose function was to swell, bluster, pick quarrels, fight duels, and guard the king's person in war. Sometimes these Orlandos would get wrought up to such a pitch of frenzy, that they would attack trees and rocks with the same indomitable bravery with which Don Quixote assailed the windmills. Depping tells us, too, that in these fits of frenzy they would eat fire, suggesting to us the origin of the fire-eaters of the present day. He tells us of two of these champions who once met in single combat, and fought till each killed the other; and even then their chivalry was not satisfied, for, tradition says, they fought long after they were dead.

Among their maxims of bravery were such as these, — never seek shelter during a tempest; never stop to dress your wounds during battle; never shed tears for the death of friends; and, when your last hour comes, be sure to die laughing. Mercy was regarded as a crime: the more blood a man had shed, the more magnificent his reception in the Hall of Odin.

We are curious to know what sort of women gave birth to such sons as these, and whether they must not have rocked their babies upon the tree-top, with the northern blast for a lullaby. Depping enlightens us a little on this point, telling us what sort of women they were, and by what courtship they were won. They, too, became sea-rovers and champions when they took the name of *Virgins of the Shield*. The more lovers a Norman maid was able to kill off in single combat, the more highly esteemed was she for her accomplishments and charms. We have a curious story of one of these accomplished maidens, a champion and a sea-rover. A suitor, more brave than the rest, chased her into the bay of Finland, boarded her skiff, met her in desperate combat, cleft her helmet in two, when she gave over, and considered herself fairly wooed and won; and the historian adds, that the conjugal felicity and endearment were more perfect and secure after a courtship like this, in which the highest virtues of both parties had been evolved.

Not far from the year 900, a revolution took place in the affairs of Norway, from which very important consequences followed, and are following still. About that time Harald (surnamed of the beautiful hair), one of the twelve kings of Norway, subdued all the rest in succession, and united the whole country under a single monarchy. He made the Scandinavian mountains his beacon summits; and if an enemy approached by sea, the nearest peak flamed with light, and flung the signal on to the next, till the whole train was ablaze from the Naze to the North Cape, and summoned every jarl to the defence of the country. Some of the jarls could not endure the tyranny of Harald, and sought refuge in other lands. Iceland was now colonized, and soon after Christianized, and became the seat of learning and civilization at a time when all Europe lay in darkness. It gave birth to a literature that still exists in the Icelandic, or native Norman language, and which, Prof. Rask of Stockholm says, rivals in copiousness, flexibility, and energy, every modern tongue.

But the most important event of this revolution in

Norway was the settlement of Normandy, in France. Rollo, a famous sea-king and pirate, was banished from Norway by Harald. He and his fire-eaters, the champions, took to their ships, and, scudding over the German sea, came down to the mouth of the Seine. There lay the province of Neustria, the most fair and goodly portion of all France, where the sunlight lay warm upon the fields, and the grapes hung luscious upon the vines. The French monarchy had become weak through internal dissensions and disorders; and so Rollo and his companions seized upon the tempting prize. This Rollo was a worthy descendant of the fire-eaters. He was surnamed The Walker, because such was his enormous stature, that every horse he mounted broke down under him, and he was obliged to travel upon his feet. They adopted the laws, the language, and the religion, of the conquered province; and the fierce sea-king and his fire-eaters became the cavaliers of Normandy, with their vassals and serfs from among the conquered people. At this time the language spoken in France was the old Latin, in its state of transition to modern French. In Northern France it was still barbarous, and was without a literature. The Norman adopted it as his own; and it soon sparkled with the brilliancy of Norman imagination, and discoursed liquid music in verse and prose. It became the language of romance; and the cavalier recounted in it his own deeds of chivalry, and the minstrel sang in it of his lady-love. The skald, who had thundered his war-odes under the ruddy flames of the northern aurora, now sang under the suns of France, his fancy still burning and sparkling with its ancient fire. The descendants of Rollo and his champions in Normandy, somewhat civilized by Christianity, became the people whence the brightest glories of chivalry took their rise. The Norman, too, had his reverence for woman; but in its development and culture it became very different from that of the Saxon.

The Norman worshipped her because she was a fair lady, with her slaves waiting around her; and then, when Giant Grim came to carry her off, it was glorious to defend her, and cleave the heads of forty giants and Saracens in the fray. The Saxon's ideal of woman culminated in the mother and the wife, who spread the charms of home around his fireside. That of the Norman culminated in my lady of Castle Hall, for one twinkle of whose eye seven knights had tilted seven days, and broke their heads in the tournament. "Her highest function," said the Norman, "is to award the prize, amid cloven mail and shivered lances." "She is in her glory," said the Saxon, "when at evening she welcomes me home from toil, her cheeks made ruddy by the blaze of the cottage fire." The first romances and tragedies were written by the Normans in Normandy;

and the most splendid works of the literature of Southern Europe were produced on the models which they had originated. The Sacred Tragedies — including the passion play — had their spirit first awakened by the minstrels who sung in the courts of Normandy. The most splendid style of modern architecture is traceable to the same origin. The Norman love of magnificence originated the Gothic cathedral, that glorious "hymn to God, sung in obedient stone." It is true, there is no trace of this in the north, where, tossing on the ocean-whirls, or ravaging the coast of his neighbor, by the dance of auroral flames, the Northman thought little of his habitation, for he needed none. But once settled in Normandy, and imbibing Christian ideas, his fervid genius was not satisfied with the demure Saxon style of houses and churches. He thought of the grand temple of nature, where Odin was worshipped on the Norwegian hills, — its myriad columns of lofty trees that made high arches together, whose organ was the winds in their eternal roar; and so the Gothic arch aspired, with its lofty windows, its clustered columns, its rows of turrets, its leaves of tracery, as if his native grove had turned to stone by the splendid magic of an enchanter.

There is a prevailing idea that people of southern countries are naturally more hot-blooded and fiery, while those of the north are phlegmatic and cold.

There is not the least truth in this notion. Native southern blood is more likely to flow in lazy and languid currents; for example, the ancient Peruvians and the Hindoos. The Norman was more of a northerner than the Saxon; and, up among his native ice and snow, he was the most fiery-brained of all men that ever lived; and the Southerner at this day owes his fire-eating capacities, not to his climate, but in spite of it, and because the blood still boils through him from his ancestry that came down from the northern pole.

The Normans had occupied Normandy about one hundred and seventy years when they invaded England. They now pass into English history, with which you are all familiar, — or, if not, you ought to be. In 1065, William, the fifth in descent from Rollo the Walker, invaded England, conquered the Saxons in the famous battle of Hastings, came to London and took possession of the government, and distributed all its important places among the officers of his army. Thus the Saxon, in his turn, was among the vanquished, and saw an aristocracy formed above him. Thus the Norman, with his imperial will and his love of grandeur, became the upper layer of the social fabric of England. The building became three stories high, — the Briton at the bottom, the Saxon in the middle, and the Norman at the top, — alas for the poor fellows who were undermost!

Our Southern States were first colonized from the top layer. Virginia was settled from a colony formed in London, made up of noblemen and titled gentry, whose prime object was to mend their worldly fortunes. There were two classes of emigrants, — criminals taken from Newgate, and called jail-birds, who were doomed to do all the manual labor; and the seventh sons of English gentry, who never labored at all. The jail-birds became the serfs of the soil; and the gentlemen became the aristocracy of Virginia and Maryland. In process of time, negroes took the place of the jail-birds; and thus the feudalism of the frozen plains of Norway, transported first to sunny France, and thence to England, crossed over the seas, and became rooted in American soil. New England was settled mainly from the middle class of English society, was an offshoot from English Saxondom, to get relief from the Norman layer that pressed grievously and heavily upon it. The sectarian divisions in England took place almost exactly according to a horizontal line, — the Norman above, and the Saxon below. The Norman above, with his splendid cathedrals, his bishops in lawn, and his gorgeous ritual; in short, the Church of England, reciting its grand old liturgy, and its organ music resounding through the arches and the long-drawn aisles, like Norwegian winds through long arcades of pine trees. The Saxon below, praying in naked conventicles, protesting against mitres and lawn as the rags of Popery, cropping out in the psalm-singing regiments of Cromwell, — those terrible image-breakers who praised God through their noses, while they rabbled cathedrals, and took the pictures of saints as wadding for their muskets. So it was, that Normandy and Saxondom came in conflict on English soil, and were thence transported beyond the main, to prolong in the latter days, and on American soil, this conflict of ages.

And with these lights of history playing about us, you will not need any explanation of the fact, that the English aristocracy fraternized with the barons of our Southern rebellion; for, depend upon it, the hatred of slavery by the English Tory is the shallowest of all delusions, and against the whole grain of his nature and history. It was not that he misunderstood the Northern cause. He understood it all too well. He knew that it was the same cause that unseated him from his place, and, in the regiments of Cromwell, broke like a volcano through the upper English layer. And you will need as little explanation of the fact that the middle layer of English life beats with us like the mighty throbs of one human heart, that its middle working-classes could not be starved into sympathy with our slaveholding rebellion, but echoed back the sentiments of Mr. Bright, with an enthusiasm that shook Exeter Hall like a new cradle of liberty. They are the same people that we are, — kith and kin with us; their hearts beat with us in '76, and through our whole war of Independence, and are always moved by the same electric thrills and touches.

The modern Yankee being of pure Saxon stock, the spirit of ancestry blows through him now as freshly as it did in the Cimbric forests. We educate him, we Christianize him, we cultivate him; but when he relapses into his inborn tastes and manners, they are as sure to be Saxon as the wave lifted up by the gale is sure to find its level when the wind has ceased to blow. The New England man of education and culture uses two languages, — one he writes and speaks in, when he wishes to put on the best appearance; and one he thinks and talks in, when he relapses into himself. We generally learn to think and talk in pure Saxon; for that is the language of the nursery. When we put on airs, we talk French and Roman; as the lady who told her folks at home that she had been reading a good book, but next day, in a fashionable and literary circle, she said she had *perused* a most delectable volume. The language we think in is the cropping out of our inmost style of mind and emotion; and the ancestral life of centuries sweeps into it, and inspires and prompts all its inflections and tones.

As Yankees, we only *guess :* when we try to show our culture, we conjecture. We love and hate right heartily in Saxon. When we get Romanized, we show our *affection* and *accession*. Mr. Emerson, by using a Saxon word instead of a Roman, branded forever an odious measure of the Democratic party. Instead of saying politely, "It will bring the country into bad odor," he said, it will make the very name of American "stink to the world;" and people held their noses from it, as if they snuffed a tainted breeze.

You are all familiar with a certain New England classic called "Mother Goose." But in the interior of New England you will seldom find any such book; but you will find the songs handed down by tradition, the unwritten lore of every household, just as Homer was preserved by the rhapsodists of Greece. And if you have ever wondered at the strange fascination which the stories have over the children, you will cease to marvel when you find that the words are nearly all Saxon, and by their very sound touch the chord of ancestral life that vibrates downward forever. Touching that chord, the sound alone wakes whole trains of thought and feeling and imagery and fantastic association; and so all sorts of odd people throng the air and the playground.

If I were to go into the nursery, and undertake to draw little folks around me with a story, I might tell them that two persons, Marcus and Portia, ascended an acclivity, to transport a vessel of water, but Marcus lost his equilibrium and fell, and fractured his cranium, and his sister experienced a similar catastrophe, and I do not think I should awaken any special interest in Marcus and Portia, even if the little people understood me perfectly well. But if I tell them, —

" Jack and Gill went up the hill, to fetch a pail of water:
Jack fell down and cracked his crown, and Gill came tumbling after,"—

I immediately clothe my hero and heroine with strange interest. Jack and Gill become famous people at once, for no other reason than that, in the latter case, I use the very language the children think, feel, laugh, and cry in.

There is yet another method of ascertaining, with a good deal of certainty, what are the hereditary tendencies of a people; and that is, by taking note of its vulgar words. There is a tendency in all of us to relapse into barbarism, for the simple reason that we belong to a stock which was lifted originally out of barbarism; and we are only held from it all the while by culture and Christianity, just as the waters of Holland are forced up out of their beds of slough by a system of pumps and dikes, and kept on a higher level, and kept clean. Let the dikes break away, and the waters go back with fearful surgings into the mire. Civilization and Christianity have lifted us up and diked us on a higher level; but in the vulgarisms of the language, we look down into a fearful Saxon slough, into which we should be sure to plunge if the dikes should give way. The vulgarisms of the language, as spoken in New England, are almost all Saxon idioms; and those who use them habitually are the native barbarians, — just such men as lived in Jutland. We will not go down far into that bathos. But go now among the rustic population, and you do not find men of *talent*, you find men of *gumption;* you do not find a man *uncultivated*, you find him a *lout* and a *loon;* boys do not get *corrected* at school, they always get *licked;* and those who made music of an evening at the town-hall did not give a concert, but tooted on their flutes, and scraped their cat-gut; and even the violin, up in the village choir, I have heard called " the Lord's fiddle." When men become very angry, and curse and swear, they always do it in pure Saxon, because then they are right earnest, and use their native tongue. When a man's indignation is factitious, and a mere show-off of oratory, he becomes Roman, and he calls the thing he hates execrable and diabolical; but when he gets right mad, and relapses into his native Saxon barbarism, he calls it damnable and devilish.

But, ladies and gentlemen, this is not all. The Saxon language, in its rudest state, was not made up chiefly of what we call vulgar words; for the good reason that Saxon life, when the most savage, had some qualities out of which the sweetest virtues and the most heavenly graces have blossomed forth. I have said that the most distinguishing characteristic of the Saxon, even in his worst state of heathenism, was reverence for woman; that he looked upon her as a superior being, and made her not only the priestess of his shrines, but the Divinity of his groves. Her virtue was more sacred than the inmost rites of the Hall of Odin; her purity more awful than the snows on the Scandinavian hills. Before Christianity came to them (long before chivalry had its rise among the Normans), this reverence for woman was the prominent feature of Saxon barbarism, and made it the sure ground for civilization to build upon after Southern Europe lay reeking in its own corruption. This sentiment is the one in which all the home virtues take root and flourish. Hence in no race is the home instinct so strong and healthful, or family relations so pure; and hence the Saxon's everlasting propensity to get a piece of land, build a house on it, and put a wife into the house, and cover all the fields about it with home memories, instead of owning his harem, or his plantation of slaves, or leading a nomadic life, and never fixing his abode. And hence you see why those words which strike deepest into our hearts, and touch the place of tears, are all Saxon words; why we laugh and cry in Saxon, but do all our shamming in Greek, Latin, and French. The names which grow out of pure and reverent love between man and woman, and the relations it creates, are all Saxon names, — *husband, wife, home, homestead, father, mother, son, daughter, child, brother, sister, lover, betrothed.* These are Saxon words sacredly appropriated, because the words which answer to these in Greek, Latin, and Oriental languages have been soiled and degraded in the corruptions of an effete civilization. For instance, to say in good Saxon, that a person has a *loving* disposition, is to pay him a compliment; but to say in Roman he has an *amorous* disposition, is a compliment you would gladly avoid. Conjugal, a Roman word, means yoked together; going down for its image to the cattle of the field. The Saxon word wife, means one that weaves (weave, woof, wife), giving you the image of woman at the loom, filling the ear with the grateful hum of home industry, and the mind with the charm of home comforts and associations. (And, by the way, I never could admire the taste of a certain class of clergymen, who always call their wives their companions, as if they never were lawfully married, but only took their meals together.) Hence you see why such a singular witchery hangs about the names which describe the homestead and the farm. Nature, before it has been humanized, we describe by Roman words.

The *mountains*, the *torrents*, the *deserts*, the *rivers*, the *plains*, the *islands*, the *continents*, and *the oceans*, — these are Roman, because they describe Nature in her wildness, and before man has covered them with heart memories and home associations. But the *farms*, the *hills*, the *streams*, the *orchards*, the *groves*, the *brooks*, the *grounds*, the *meadows*, the *gardens*, and the *bowers*, — these are all Saxon, for they are fragrant with domestic sympathies and loves. There is a house near by them, and in sight, with lights gleaming through its windows, "where the busy housewife plies her evening care." The great fowls of the air, that are birds of prey, and never domesticate, — the *eagles*, the *herons*, and the *vultures*, — have Roman names; but the *doves*, the *sparrows*, the *swallows*, the *bobolinks*, the *larks*, the *wrens*, the *chickadees*, that pick the crumbs from your door, and twitter under your eaves, and wake you by their minstrelsy of a summer morning, — these are pure Saxon, for they catch the home instinct, and reflect its loves. And the *robin*, though his first name is Roman, yet owes his addition of *redbreast* to the same gentle and loving characteristic. He takes his surname from the Saxon, because he builds his nest and sings in the old apple-tree beside your door. So it is that the pure old Saxon sentiment of reverence for woman, *as woman*, became the stem out of which the domestic virtues blossomed forth, and threw their sweetest fragrancy and beauty about the homestead, after the Roman empire had gone down in the mire, and the relations between its men and women were polluted with lust. And the Saxon sentiment has thrown enchantment over all things within its sphere, and made them haunt our memories with strange and witching music. As a living poet says, very beautifully, —

" Old Saxon words, old Saxon words, your spells are round us thrown :
Ye haunt our daily paths and dreams with a music all your own.
Each one, in its own power a host, to fond remembrance brings
The earliest, brightest aspect back of life's familiar things.

Yours are the *hills*, the *fields*, the *woods*, the *orchards*, and the *streams*,
The *meadows* and the *bowers*, that bask in the sun's rejoicing beams :
'Mid them our childhood's years were kept, our childhood's thoughts were reared,
And by your household tones its joys were evermore endeared.

We have roamed since then where the myrtle bloomed in its own unclouded realms,
But our hearts return with changeless love to the brave old Saxon ELMS ;
Where the laurel o'er its native streams of a deathless glory spoke,
But we passed with pride to the later fame of the sturdy Saxon OAK."

For similar reasons, the Saxon courage became something very different from the brute ferocity of other savages. The Highland Celt fought from fealty to his chieftain and his clan, and from his innate love of brutality and blood. The Saxon fought for land, — land to put his house on; and, having put a wife into it, he fought for his home; and that breathed into his courage a sublimer sentiment, and lifted it above the ferocity of the animal.

Hence the arts of peace flourish pre-eminently under Saxon rule. Nobody but a Yankee understands the full correlative meaning of those two words, liberty and law. Saxon civilization is peaceful. Norman is warlike. Our military terms are for the most part Roman words; for these are used to functions of government and conquest, and breathe the spirit of the battle-field. On the other hand, the Saxon words take their flavor from the household, and preserve its aroma, and spring a long train of memories after them. As Mr. Macaulay says of reading Milton, the words suggest a great deal more than they mean, and carry you back to your childhood, to the schoolroom, by some magic you cannot analyze. None knew better than Milton the secret of this word-magic. In his controversial prose works he builds up Latin sentences whole pages high, and rolls them down upon his enemies like Jupiter launching from Olympus his thunder volleys, which keep on growling and growling till they get half way round the sky. But open "Paradise Lost," and if you come to a passage that haunts you with its witching music, and calls back the hours when you walked with your betrothed by moonlight, or when you went in rosy childhood to drive the cattle, brushing the dews from the grass, and hearing the birds sing to the sunrise, I venture to say that two-thirds of the words are Saxon, and for that reason have become flavored with the home affections.

Here is a sentence of eighty-nine words; and just seventy-two of them are Saxon: —

> "With thee conversing I forget all time;
> All seasons, and their change, all please alike.
> Sweet is the breath of morn, her rising sweet,
> With charm of earliest birds: pleasant the sun,
> When first on this delightful land he spreads
> His orient beams, on herb, tree, fruit, and flower,
> Glistening with dew; fragrant the fertile earth
> After soft showers; and sweet the coming on
> Of grateful evening mild; then silent night,
> With this her solemn bird, and this fair moon,
> And these the gems of heaven, her starry train."

Saxon superstitions, such as existed more than one thousand years ago in Jutland, have even come down to us, and are alive to-day in New England; for example, those about the moon, and about lucky and unlucky days. Mr. Turner says any peasant *now* would be ashamed of them. He is mistaken. Off in Berkshire County, which is of pure native stock, a farmer one day was crossing his neighbor's fields, and saw him with a bag of grain, sitting down, and waiting patiently for the lucky hour of sowing.

"What are you waiting for?" said his neighbor.

"For ten minutes past two," said he.

"And what is to happen then?"

"Why, the moon changes." He would not sow ten minutes before, for fear of losing his crop. The same man probably would not undertake a journey on Friday, or Freda's Day, nor crawl under a bar without spitting back, to take off the evil charm. If a child is born on such a day, it will live; on such other day, it will die. Whatever you dream, on the first night of the old moon, will be joyful to you; and your luck for the month depends upon your seeing the new moon on your right hand. If you dream of seeing an eagle fly over your head, you will be promoted, — how high depends on the height of the eagle. Charms for the cure of disease were numerous; and a man told me once that he relieved his rheumatism by one of these charms, and, if I should describe it, I am afraid you would not believe me. And the same methods of divination for discerning the future, practised in Jutland more than one thousand years ago, are good in some parts of New England even till this day.

But we have not time to explore this mine, though a very fertile one.

What is to be the issue in America, of this long conflict between the Saxon and the Norman, is a question already decided. It was decided even before our civil war, which crippled the Norman, and shattered his institutions in pieces. Glance for an instant over the map, and measure with your eye the vast unsettled territory of the United States. It extends through eighteen degrees of latitude, and occupies both slopes of the Rocky Mountains, — one slope stretching east, to the Mississippi; the other west, to the Pacific Sea. Its space is equal to all the twenty-five States east of the Mississippi. It has all the climates of all the zones, and extends through the realms of perpetual frost and perpetual flowers; its rivers more majestic than those of the East; its soil the richest in all the world, — richer in gold than the sands of Pactolus; its trees, whether for beauty or for use, of more value, a thousand times, than those that "weep amber on the banks of Po." The whole eastern part of this region is underlaid with coal-mines; and there one day will be, not only the granaries, but the workshops and manufactories of the world. In the coming century, the seat of commerce is to be transferred to the western shore. Into that region the United States are moving at the rate of seventeen miles a year. And it is a most interesting fact, that the Northern tide outstrips the Southern, as two to one ; carrying with it New England institutions and ideas. There is no law of nature which forbids serfdom there, for it existed on the Norwegian hills : but there is a law of God that will exclude it ; and that is the omnipotence of the family institution, over feudalism with its elements of weakness and decay; and thus the Saxon home is sure to cover these western slopes with its sweet associations and memories, and make the whole range of the Rocky Mountains echo with the music of the Saxon tongue.

# POEMS.

# EMANCIPATION.

HARK! through the North a SPIRIT waking slow,
And rousing like a strong man after sleep:
Its murmurs come like whirlwinds speaking low,
Ere yet they lift the billows of the deep.
What though this power is long and slow to wake!
Oh! ye are mad, its strength to brave and dare;
For, if its thunders from their mountains wake,
They'll smite your fields, and clear the northern air.
Then from the North, along its whole frontier,
A light shall stream in columns to the skies,
And like a new Aurora shall appear
To the whole land that South in darkness lies:
And while its flames do shake their banners near,
Your slaves will hail them with rejoicing eyes.

1844.

# "OLD JOHN BROWN."

THEY call thee hot-brained, crazed, and mad;
    But every word that falls
Goes straight and true, and hits the mark
    More sure than cannon-balls.
Through spectre forms of bogus law
    It cuts its way complete:
And judge and jury, too, are tried
    At God's great judgment-seat.


Old man, farewell! They'll take thy life:
    For dangerous enough,
In these our sweetly piping times,
    Are men of hero stuff.
We should tread soft above the fires
    That underneath us lie:
You'll crack the crust of compromise,
    And set them spouting high.


Where Henry's cry for "Liberty"
    Once sent its shivering thrill,
There's only room, six feet by two,
    For heroes now to fill.
And o'er the spot the years will roll,
    As spring its verdure weaves,
And autumn o'er the felon's grave
    Shakes down its yellow leaves.

But not the spot six feet by two
    Will hold a man like thee:
John Brown will tramp the shaking earth
    From Blue Ridge to the sea,
Till the strong angel comes at last,
    And ope's each dungeon door,
And God's Great Charter holds, and waves
    O'er all his humble poor.

And then the humble poor will come,
    In that far distant day,
And from the felon's nameless grave
    They'll brush the leaves away;
And gray old men will point the spot,
    Beneath the pine-tree shade,
As children ask with streaming eyes,
    Where Old John Brown was laid.

NOVEMBER, 1859.

# SONG OF THE STARS AND STRIPES.

WE see the gallant streamer yet
    Float from the bastioned walls:
One hearty song for fatherland
    Before its banner fails!
Last on our gaze when, outward bound,
    We plough the ocean's foam;
First on our longing eyes again,
    To waft our welcome home.

Beneath thy shade we've toiled in peace,
    The golden corn we reap;
We've taken home our bonny brides,
    We've rocked our babes to sleep;
We marched to front the battle storms
    That brought the invader nigh,
When the grim lion cowered and sank
    Beneath the eagle's eye.

Beneath the stars and stripes we'll keep,
    Come years of weal or woe:
Close up again the broken line,
    And let the traitors go!
Ho, brothers of the "Border States"!
    We reach across the line,
And pledge our faith and honor now,
    As once in Auld Lang Syne.

We'll keep the memories bright and green
    Of all our old renown;
We'll strike the traitor hand that's raised
    To pluck the eagle down.
Still shall it guard your Southern homes
    From all the foes that come:
We'll move with you to harp and flute,
    Or march to fife and drum.

Or, if ye turn from us in scorn,
    Still shall our nation's sign
Roll out again its streaming stars
    On all the border line.
And with the same old rallying cry,
    Beneath its folds we'll meet:
And they shall be our conquering sign,
    Or be our winding-sheet!

'Tis said that when Jerusalem
    Sank in her last despair,
A spectre sword hung gory red
    Just o'er her in the air.
Ye that tear down your country's flag,
    Look, where God's gathering ire
Hangs in its place, just o'er your heads,
    A sword of bloody fire!

MARCH, 1861.

# SONG FOR JULY 4, 1861.

STILL wave our streamer's glorious folds
    O'er all the brave and true,
Though ten dim stars have turned to blood
    On yonder field of blue.

It is our nation's judgment-day,
    That makes her stars to fall.
Lo! all the dead start from their graves
    At Freedom's trumpet-call.

And in the thunders of the storm
    She speaks, an angel strong:
"Now comes my reign of righteousness:
    Now ends the slavers' wrong.

Lift up your heads, ye faithful ones,
    For now your prayers prevail.
Ye faithless! hear the tramp of doom,
    And dread the iron hail!

God's last Messiah comes apace
    In Freedom's awful name,
And parts the tribes to right and left, —
    To glory or to shame."

Then wave the streamer's glorious folds
    O'er all the brave and true,
Till all its stars shine bright again
    On yonder field of blue.

# THE HOME GUARD.

ON the nations bound in error,
    Lies the ancient night of terror,—
Lies the old Egyptian gloom.
Still the blinded nations leading,
Are the hosts of martyrs bleeding,—
    Bleeding till the morning come.

Where the stars and stripes are streaming,
Fall the martyrs, grandly dreaming
    Of the coming Age of Gold;
And we write their names in glory,
Fighting in the battle gory,
    Lying in their coffins cold.

But those other martyrs' praises,
Which no trump of fame upraises,
    But whose works their glory show,—
Parents, teachers, wives, and daughters,
Leading by the gentle waters
    Where the trees of knowledge grow,—

Faithful Home Guard of the nation,
In its glorious celebration
    Shall your works forever shine;
For they break the night of terror,
And drive back the ancient error,
    Leading in the Day Divine.

JULY 4, 1861.

# HOW GOLD MAY BE KEPT BRIGHT.

[From Horace.]

O CRISPUS, foe to sordid gain!
   The man whose heart is tender
Makes all the gold his hands obtain
   Shine with redoubled splendor.

Thus Proculeius lives in song,
   And all our love engages:
Fame bears him on her wings along
   The never-dying ages.

For when, upon his brothers, Fate
   With cruel hand was pressing,
He shared with them his own estate,
   With all a father's blessing.

Add field to field, — rule all the climes
   Whose shores the sea is laving:
'T is nobler far to rule betimes
   The soul that's in thee craving.

# GOLDEN MEAN.

[Translation.  Horace, Carmen X., Lib. II.]

WHILE the fierce winds above us sweep,
    Let us, my friend, our vessel keep
Not on the wide and surging deep,
    Nor near the treacherous shoals.
To whom the golden medium falls,
He dwelleth not in ruined walls,
Nor proudly walks in splendid halls,
    The mark of envious souls.

Huge pines by fiercest blasts are blown,
The loftiest towers come heaviest down,
On skyward cliffs so bleak and brown
    The thunderbolt will ring.
So let us fear 'mid fortune's blaze,
And let us hope in evil days:
Winter recedes, and o'er his ways
    Dance the gay hours of spring.

The ills of life shall then retire:
Apollo sometimes strikes his lyre
To joyous notes; nor in his ire
    Doth always bend his bow.
Therefore, amid thy troubles here,
Bear bravely up with lofty cheer;
And slack thy sails, and wisely fear,
    When prosperous breezes blow.

MAY, 1851.

# SERENITY.

[A paraphrase from Horace. Carmen III., Lib. II.]

MY friend, where'er you tread this scene
    Of varied joys and cares,
Preserve thy mind alike serene
    In sad or gay affairs.

Whether you live in sorrow's shade,
    Or on the grass recline
In bowers by pines and poplars made
    To quaff the generous wine, —

There, while the boughs above thy head
    A living roof weave high,
And purling brooks with quivering tread
    Run bounding gladly by, —

Let them bring wine, and sweet perfume,
    And roses fresh and gay;
For soon, like these, we cease to bloom,
    And fade from earth away.

The house, the grove, the costly field
    Which yellow Tiber laves,
This heaped-up wealth to heirs we yield,
    And seek forgotten graves.

## SERENITY.

The highest and the humblest thing,
    The wealthiest, poorest, — all
Are victims to the tyrant king,
    And all alike must fall.

Even now the fatal lot we know
    Is shaken in the urn:
Soon it comes forth, and then we go
    Whence we shall not return.

May, 1851.

## OLD ENGLAND AND NEW.

[Written and sung on board the Cunard steamship "Siberia," which sailed from Liverpool Aug. 20, 1873.]

OLD ENGLAND's shore of summer green
    Fades on the dark-blue waters.
God's blessing on thy noble Queen,
    And all thy sons and daughters!
The land where holy martyrs bled,
    Of thrilling song and story, —
Thy sun shines bright, and may it shed
    A blaze of endless glory!


Land of the western shore! we keep
    Our filial hearts still near thee:
Our love for thee grows strong and deep,
    With all our wanderings weary.
Above our homes thy peaceful bow
    Its sweetest hues is blending;
Thy lightnings round the world that go,
    Not bane, but bliss, are sending.


Our gallant ship that walks the seas
    From one shore to the other,
Oh, bear the olive-boughs of peace
    From brother back to brother!

God bless thy captain and his men,
The waves thy pathway making.
And all who keep the golden chain
Of brotherhood from breaking!

# ODE.

[For the fiftieth anniversary of Dr. Eliphalet Nott's Presidency at Union College, Schenectady.]

"We've wandered east, we've wandered west,"
   Since through these halls we strayed
And fondly dreamed our waking dreams
   In Union's soothing shade.
Now we return with sandals worn,
   To Learning's ancient shrine
Where busy memories start and throng
   From days of auld lang syne, —
The thronging memories fond and dear
      Of auld lang syne.

We've wandered east, we've wandered west,
   On prairie, sea, and shore ;
And some have laid their weary forms
   Where life's last dream is o'er.
They walked with us through Learning's bowers,
   And plucked its " gowans fine : "
They girded on their armor bright,
   With us in days lang syne.
We'll breathe for them one pensive strain
      Of auld lang syne.

We've wandered east, we've wandered west,
   O'er many a shifting scene :
This spot, in all the lengthening past,
   Has only grown more green ;

For here our father, friend and sage,
    With locks of silvery shine,
Kept watch above our youthful ways,
    In days of auld lang syne.
We've kept his memory bright and dear
       Of auld lang syne.

Borne onward by the solemn sea,
    From time's receding shore,
Union, thy light, from which we steered,
    Shall greet our eyes no more.
Still thou, the Pharos of the waves,
    Shalt o'er the waters shine,
And bear upon thy beaming front
    One name from years lang syne, —
One ever dear remembered name.
       Of auld lang syne.

# HYMN.

[Written for, and sung at the ordination of Mr. Sears, in Wayland, Feb. 20, 1839.]

OUR fathers, where are they,
   Who here in ancient time
Came with the faltering steps of age,
   Or manhood's glorious prime?
Oh! some in yonder peaceful tombs
   Their long, last sabbath keep,
Where from the idle, hurrying throng
   The mourner turns to weep.

Along these solemn aisles
   Where floats the song of praise,
Do not their lingering spirits hear
   Their old and cherished lays?
And when the fervent voice of prayer
   To God for favor calls,
Oh! blend they not their spirit tones
   That "talk along the walls"?

Their children, where are they,
   Who now their footsteps tread?
Walk they in bonds of love and peace,
   To join the pious dead?
Come blooming youth, come reverend age,
   While yet your years revolve,
And take, within this holy fane,
   The high and pure resolve.

God of our fathers, hear
    The solemn vows we pay,
And let celestial breathings move
    Upon our souls to-day !
Oh, may the tie we consecrate,
    Thy pledge of favor prove !
Shed here thy warm, benignant beams
    Of everlasting love.

# HYMN.

[For the fiftieth anniversary of the settlement of Rev. Joseph Field, D D., over the First Parish in Weston.]

FATHER of mercies! in the radiant morning
    Thy youthful servant started on his way:
And prayers were breathed for light and grace adorning,
    And that his strength be equal to his day.

And Thou hast answered. Fifty years of blessing
    Have fallen o'er us gently as the rain:
Thy promised grace, thy heavenly peace, possessing,
    Here in thy house, and in our homes again.

Father, we thank Thee. Through the fruitful meadows,
    Still guide the flock and pastor by thy hand,
And grant him, walking through the evening shadows,
    Still brighter openings towards the Promised Land,

Till, passing on through earth's brief joys and trials,
    Pastor and people join the immortal throng,
Who sweeter incense waft from golden vials,
    And worship Thee in their unending song.

FEBRUARY, 1865.

# GOLDEN-WEDDING HYMN.

TWO summer streams were flowing
    Bright in the morning sun;
And in their course, with gentle force,
    They mingled into one.[1]

Now flows the blended river
    Beneath the western sky;
And manifold the hues of gold
    Calm on its bosom lie.

So, friends beloved and honored,
    Your stream of life has flowed;
And now may rest upon its breast
    The golden peace of God!

Warm hearts are beating round you;
    And in our fervent song,
Here do we pray, your closing day
    May linger late and long;

That warmest benedictions
    May soothe its latest stage,
And wreathe with flowers of summer hours
    The snowy crown of age;

---

[1] The opening stanza is not a literal quotation, but is in close imitation of Brainard's very beautiful Epithalamium, commencing, —

    "I saw two clouds at morning."

Till, clothed in wedding garments,
    You stand before the throne
Whence cometh down the bridal crown,
    And the sweet voice, "WELL DONE!"

1865.

# A GREETING FROM THE SUNDAY SCHOOL.

[Written for the Christmas Festival of the Sunday School at Weston, Dec. 25, 1875.]

HO, teachers, friends, and parents dear,
    Who join our festive throng,
We send you greeting as we sing
    Our merry Christmas song!
The song which here we sing to-night
    Shall be the glad refrain
Of that which swept the heavenly lyres
    O'er Bethlehem's starlit plain.

O ye whose selfish hearts are chilled
    Beneath the world's cold blight,
Make room! make room! for lo! He comes —
    A Saviour comes to-night.
Hold up to Him your waning lamps,
    To fill with oil once more,
Till, from the fount of Love Divine,
    Your souls are brimming o'er.

And ye who bear the ills of life,
    And faint beneath its load,
Grown weary of your painful toil
    To climb the heavenly road,

Good cheer! good cheer! He comes — He comes,
    Your pain and grief to share;
For He who reigns in glory now
    Has borne the cross ye bear.


Ho, children! sing, and clap your hands,
    And lift your notes of praise
To Him whose heart beats warm with yours,
    In childhood's winsome ways.
He came your joyous times to know, —
    The babe of heavenly birth;
For He who reigns in glory now
    Was once a child on earth.


Hail, Santa Claus! whose hand to-night
    Brings tokens rich and free:
The fruits that grow in sunniest climes
    Hang on the Christmas-tree.
Good-will and Faith and Hope and Love
    Its bending branches bear.
Come, let us pluck the healing leaves
    And golden clusters there.

# CALM AT SEA.

[Off Cohasset Beach, July 8, 1847.]

YE spirits of the air and wave,
   Oh! whither are ye fled?
All nature sleeps; nor only sleeps,
   But, like a corpse, lies dead.
Across the charmed and glassy sea
   No morning zephyr strays:
The sun, with face of blood-red hue,
   Looks angry through the haze.

The sky above, and the sky below,
   With rival fires are seen;
And midway in this awful space
   Our vessel hangs between.
But we move! not o'er the heaving main,
   Where cool sea-breezes blow,
But we're sinking down, we're sinking down,
   To lodge in that sky below.

---

Look yonder! for some spectre moves
   In terror o'er the sea:
Beneath his wings the waves look black,
   And quiver frightfully.
He comes! he comes! our vessel scuds
   Before his threatening ire;
And from our prow, on either side,
   Roll floods of foaming fire.

He smites the air, and from their cells
    Rush out the shrieking gales :
They catch the canvas as they come,
    And flap the bellying sails.
Across the noon his ghastly form
    Its baleful shadow flings :
He lifts the spray, and through the air
    He shakes it from his wings.

Ah, treacherous calm! like that which comes
    O'er souls that sleep in sin,
What time the passions cease to stir,
    And stillness reigns within.
I thought my sins removed; I felt
    Their power within me die :
I thought the peace of souls redeemed
    Came sweetly from on high.

And then, alas! they woke again,
    And raged without control :
Storms that had seemed forever hushed
    Swept o'er my darkened soul ;
O'er the dead waves of deep desire
    Some dark temptation came ;
And so my bark was tossed again
    On waves of rolling flame.

Methinks that on this solemn scene,
    And at this thoughtful hour,
Where ever-changing forms do preach
    God's never-changing power;

## CALM AT SEA.

While from the quickly pulsing waves,
    The loud sea-anthems roll, —
A more prevailing prayer might rise
    From the heavenward breathing soul : —


Send then, O God, thy cherubim
    All fragrant with thy love,
And let their whitely-flashing wings
    Around my spirit move ;
There let them breathe no treacherous calm,
    But breathe a holy rest
Till thy glorious heavens see themselves
    In my clear and tranquil breast.

# DIRGE.

FAREWELL, brother! deep and lowly
    Rest thee on thy bed of clay.
Kindred saints, and angels holy,
    Bore thy heavenward soul away.
Sad, we gave thee to that number
    Laid in yonder icy halls,
Where above thy peaceful slumber
    Many a shower of sorrow falls.


Hear our prayer, O God of glory,
    Lowly breathed in sorrow's song!
Bleeding hearts lie bare before Thee,
    Come, in holy trust made strong.
Hark! a voice moves nearer, stronger,
    From the shadowy land ye dread, —
"Mortals! mortals! seek no longer
    Those that live, among the dead."


Farewell, brother! soon we meet thee
    Where no cloud of sorrow rolls;
For glad tidings float, how sweetly!
    From the glorious land of souls.
Death's cold gloom — it parts asunder:
    Lo! the folding shades are gone.
Mourner, upward! yonder, yonder,
    "God's broad day comes pouring on!"

# GUARDIAN ANGELS.

[Written by the bedside of a very sick lady, who seemed in a sweet sleep.]

AS in the garden's gloomy shades,
   To Jesus bending low,
They came, and from his burdened soul
   Rolled off its weight of woe;
So now they come whene'er we droop
   With sickness, care, or pain,
And pour a cool, assuaging balm
   Through every burning vein.

At night I seek my weary couch,
   Now rough with many a thorn,
And pray, while sleep forsakes my eyes,
   "Oh, speed the wings of morn!"
But ere the light from morning land
   First through my window gleams,
The guardian spirit softly comes,
   And prompts my pleasing dreams.

When the frail robe thy spirit wears,
   At length is worn away,
The angel band shall lead thee on,
   And smooth thine upward way;
And thou wilt rise, thou weary one,
   And be an angel too,
And bear the same sweet ministries
   Which now they bear to you.

# IN SICKNESS.

There is an hour of silent prayer:
    I've felt its joys serene,
When, Lord, thy face beamed like a sun,
    With not a cloud between:
'Twas when my passions lulled to rest,
    And all my pride was still,
Thy peace descended as the dew
    Falls soft on Hermon's hill.


If here amidst the storms of life,
    Shut in this house of clay,
Such gleams of glory struggle through
    From thine eternal day,
Oh, what the peace that o'er the heart
    Its golden dews distils,
Beneath that morn that ever reigns
    O'er all the heavenly hills!


But here the clouds will cast their gloom
    Across my sunlit skies:
Dark thoughts, like flocks of evil birds,
    Out of my heart will rise.
And yet I know thine angels come,
    An ever-shining throng,
To guard from evil, and to make
    My spirit bright and strong.

Lord, send thy pure, baptizing fire
  To cleanse my heart anew;
And o'er my spirit let thy grace
  Descend like heavenly dew.
Come as thy Spirit came of old,
  Soft on the rushing breeze,
And fit me for those " heavenly troops
  And sweet societies."

JULY 19, 1847.

# AWAY FROM CHURCH.

FATHER Divine! thy glorious face,
    That beamed so bright erewhile,
Now seems behind the gathering clouds
    To hide its gracious smile.
How heavy o'er my couch of care
    These sabbath hours have flown!
Far from the meekly gathering flock,
    Their pastor droops alone.


'Tis not the sufferings Thou dost send,
    'Tis not the pain I bear,
That hangs upon my drooping heart
    This heavy load of care;
'Tis not the opening gate of death,
    The Christian's sweet release,
Through which thy beckoning angel calls
    Up to the land of peace.


But while those sweetly sounding chimes
    Here through my windows roll,
Thy word, that must not pass my lips,
    Lies burning in my soul.
And oh! another thought than that
    Comes o'er my spirit now,
Deepening the shade that sickness flings
    Across my throbbing brow.

## AWAY FROM CHURCH.

For ere the cheek had lost its glow,
   Or the arm had lost its power,
Oh! did I serve Thee as I ought,
   And seize the golden hour?
Mine was the sorrowing to console,
   The sinful to reprove;
Did I give my people all my strength
   And undivided love?


Now, too, the Past throws wide its doors,
   As Memory turns the key,
And shows how poor are all the works
   My hands have done for Thee.
Then up, and up, through golden air,
   While the earth wanes below,
I see thy saints, that cast their crowns,
   In white robes bending low.


How glad they move on wingèd feet,
   Thy mandates to fulfil!
No self in them to be denied, —
   Theirs but the Eternal Will.
Oh! in these long and silent hours,
   Send thy baptizing love,
That I on earth may do thy will,
   As they in heaven above.


Oh! now I see a Father's love,
   And not a Father's frown:
Thou mak'st the burning tongue be still,
   And the hands hang feebly down.

For in thy name the tongue must speak,
   And in that name alone;
That feeble hand thy glory serve,
   But never serve its own.

My God! thy high and pure designs
   I seek not to explore:
Thine is my strength if here restored,
   Thine when my life is o'er.
Thine through these lingering days I'll live,
   And thine in meekness die;
And in my Father's folding arms,
   Now like a child I lie.

1862.

# "SHOW US THE FATHER."

SHOW us the Father! Lift thine eye
   And bend thy gaze above,
Where, mild and clear, the evening star
   Sends down its look of love;
When sinking Day resigns once more
   The fields he brightly won,
And Night, with slow and solemn pomp,
   O'er her wide realm moves on.


Show us the Father! Now the sun
   Sinks in his "golden grave,"
And weary whirlwinds droop their wings
   Upon the peaceful wave.
The land and sea unite to raise
   Their grateful evening hymn;
While Nature's altar-fires burn bright,
   Devotion's fire burns dim.


Show us the Father! Beauty flings
   Her banner on the air,
And Earth, from all her sombre heights,
   Sends up her evening prayer.
Summer's low anthems sweetly breathe
   From harps of heavenly frame:
Comes there no sound upon thine ear,
   To speak the Father's name?

## "SHOW US THE FATHER."

Oh! if the earth-bound spirit feels
    No presence from above,
Turn to that everlasting page,
    Bright with a Father's love.
Close the wide world of glory out,
    Of sea and earth and air;
And, having shut thy closet door,
    Oh! meet the Father there.

1836.

## TWO SPIRIT WORLDS.

"THERE is a land of pure delight,
   Where saints immortal reign;"
Their saintly minds in heaven's pure light
   Cleave not to earth again.

No winter storms in their abode,
   No blight, and no decay:
Their sunshine is the smile of God,
   That makes eternal day.

How young they grow, as o'er them still
   The endless years roll on!
How strong they grow to do God's will,
   And live to Him alone!

Another spirit land, I trow,
   Vexed with our mean affairs,
Lies close upon earth's confines low,
   And meddles with its cares.

The "carnal mind" still to them clings,
   Is with them there as here;
And so, with endless gossipings,
   They mingle in our sphere.

Friend of my youth! who here in time
   Put on thy robes of white,
Thy home is on those heights sublime,
   Among the sons of Light.

Not mingling in our vulgar noise,
    Thy cheery tones we hear,
But mingling in the " still small voice "
    That charms my inward ear.

JULY 30, 1875.

# MY PSALM.

O THOU most present in our paths
    When least thy steps we see!
Amid these wrecks of earthly hopes
    I breathe my prayer to Thee.

What though this house thy hand has built
    Must in these ruins fall!
My soul shall rise, sustained by Thee,
    Serene above them all.

And pain, which in the long, long hours
    Keeps on by night and day,
Through these fast crumbling walls to Thee
    Finds a new opening way;

For through the rents already made,
    I see thy glorious face,
And songs unheard by mortal ears
    Chant thy redeeming grace.

Oh! build anew this mortal frame,
    And make it serve Thee still,
Or make these ministries of pain
    Their blessed end fulfil,

That, held and chastened by thy hand,
    I yet may come to Thee,
Subdued and ripened for the work
    Of immortality.

For there upon the immortal shores,
 The throngs in white array
Came from these ministries of pain,
 To serve Thee night and day.

June 18, 1875.

www.ingramcontent.com/pod-product-compliance
Lightning Source LLC
Chambersburg PA
CBHW032054230426
43672CB00009B/1595